W9-ATS-823

FE '08

that's Life

finding scrapbook inspiration in the everyday

Nic Howard

WITHDRAWN

Memory Makers Books
Cincinnati, Ohio

www.memorymakersmagazine.com

Mount Laurel Library
100 Walt Whitman Avenue
Mount Laurel, NJ 08054-9539
856-234-7319
www.mtlaurel.lib.nj.us

That's Life. Copyright © 2007 by Nic Howard. Manufactured in China. All rights reserved. No part of this book may be reproduced in any form or by any electronic or mechanical means including information storage and retrieval systems without permission in writing from the publisher, except by a reviewer who may quote brief passages in a review. Published by Memory Makers Books, an imprint of F+W Publications, Inc., 4700 East Galbraith Road, Cincinnati, Ohio, 45236. (800) 289-0963. First edition.

11 10 09 08 07   5 4 3 2 1

Distributed in Canada by Fraser Direct
100 Armstrong Avenue
Georgetown, ON, Canada L7G 5S4
Tel: (905) 877-4411

Distributed in the U.K. and Europe by David & Charles
Brunel House, Newton Abbot, Devon, TQ12 4PU, England
Tel: (+44) 1626 323200, Fax (+44) 1626 323319
E-mail: postmaster@davidandcharles.co.uk

Distributed in Australia by Capricorn Link
P.O. Box 704, S. Windsor, NSW 2756 Australia
Tel: (02) 4577-3555

Library of Congress Cataloging-in-Publication Data

That's life : finding scrapbook inspiration in the everyday / by Nic Howard. -- 1st ed.
    p. cm.
  Includes index.
  ISBN-13: 978-1-59963-001-4 (pbk. : alk. paper)
  ISBN-10: 1-59963-001-X (pbk. : alk. paper)
  1. Photographs--Conservation and restoration. 2. Scrapbook journaling. 3. Scrapbooks. I. Title.
TR465.H72 2007
745.593--dc22

                              2007007209

Editor: Karen Davis
Designer: Marissa Bowers
Layout Artist: Kelly O'Dell
Art Coordinator: Eileen Aber
Production Coordinator: Matt Wagner
Photographers: Christine Polomsky; John Carrico, Adam Henry,
            Adam Leigh-Manuell, Alias Imaging LLC
Photo Stylist: Nora Martini

Digital images courtesy of Katie Pertiet, www.designerdigitals.com.

About the Author

Nic Howard lives in New Zealand with her husband and three children. She discovered scrapbooking in 1999, after the arrival of her first child, and never looked back. Nic's first page was published in 2000. Her largest scrapbooking accomplishment came in 2005 when she became one of ten winners in the Memory Makers Masters competition. Since then, Nic's work has appeared in numerous books and scrapbooking magazines. These days you will find Nic in her scrap room creating projects for one of several manufacturer design teams or working on freelance assignments.

Dedication

For Shauna, who has always guided me along my scrapbooking path.

And for my children, who are my constant inspiration.

Acknowledgements

The last six months have certainly been a crazy ride. I have so many people to thank for keeping me sane.

Thank you to my children, Jacob, Braden and Abby, who provided me with so much inspiration and material for this book. I love you dearly.

To my husband, Paul, who supported me all the way; when things were tough you always found the perfect rugby league analogy to encourage me. "You have broken through the defence; you have sidestepped the full-back. Don't drop the ball now!" I didn't drop the ball. It's a touch down. I love you.

To Mum and Dad. Thanks for being there, for realizing how much I wanted this and for being an endless help to make sure it happened.

To my friends. Thanks for your patience, your understanding and your support as my book world temporarily consumed me.

To the artists who believed in me enough to contribute their own beautiful artwork.

To Christine Doyle, for all of your help and advice while I compiled the proposal and completed the book process.

To Memory Makers Books for the opportunity to share my everyday inspiration the way I wanted to.

And finally the last thank you has to go to the last banana, Continental quick dinners, dairy milk chocolate and the "Charlie and the Chocolate Factory" DVD. All of which are the everyday ordinary things I will always remember as I read this book.

Contents

Introduction

Telling the **story** has always been important to me. From childhood days, where as an eight-year-old I wrote and colored in my journal, to today, where I communicate the stories in my scrapbook pages, the words and the details I want to convey have always been my motivation to create.

The conversation included on "The Last Banana" layout (page 11) really happened. My husband and I actually stood in the kitchen and chatted about what would happen to that last banana in the fruit bowl. We began to laugh as we imagined the result if the banana was given to our two-year-old daughter. Tears of laughter rolled down our faces as we talked about how the banana would feel if it was subjected to my cooking skills. "I bet you turn that into a scrapbook page," Paul said, as we finished laughing. "Darn right, I will," I replied. I love turning this type of everyday stuff into scrapbook pages. It's fun. It's the things we don't always remember a week or a month later, and yet it is the essence of our everyday life. I'd love to see more of these types of layouts around. And with that, the idea to write this book was planted in my mind.

Some of my favorite layouts in my albums are the ones others seem to love too. They are the pages that cause people to stop, smile and say, "I would never have thought to do a layout about that!" or "I need to do a page about this aspect of my day." Well, now is the time to start. Let's get down to the simple stuff. Look at your albums and check how you tell the real day-to-day stories. Listen to the people around you and ask yourself if your pages reflect their true personalities. Write down conversations with family and friends and include them in your artwork.

This book features a collection of my own pages, created from my everyday experiences, as well as pages by a few contributing artists. You may or may not have similar experiences, but I'm sure you will be able to relate to the humor, the fun, the daily tasks and even the personal feelings. I'm telling my story and I hope that in reading this book you will be inspired to look behind the big events in your life to scrap the little things that tell your story. Because it is the little things that will let people know, in years to come, who we really were.

THE LAST Banana...

- LEFT UNTIL THE SPOTS TAKE OVER AND BEING THROWN AWAY.
- BANANA MUFFINS (OK SO NOT LIKELY)
- BEING PUT IN A LUNCH BOX ONLY TO BE RETURNED IN A WORSE STATE (AND ULTIMATELY BEING THROWN AWAY).
- BEING GRABBED BY THE TODDLER-MONSTER, PARTIALLY EATEN AND THE REMAINDER SMASHED AROUND THE PLACE.
- JUST SOME OF THE THINGS PAUL & I CAME UP WITH,
- IN A TOTALLY RANDOM BUT AWESOMELY FUNNY CONVERSATION WE HAD TODAY.

July '06

and smoke cigarettes all the way [to your] destination and you were given rea[l ...] You could take whatever you liked [on the] plane. The freedom of a pre-9.1[1 ...] How innocent we were. I'm not su[re the] travel plans we had are still in p[lace. It] saddens me, but who knows what th[e ...] will be like by the time we save [...] money to board that plane. I talk[ed to a] friend recently who was travelling [to] the U.S.A. after visiting here. The [security] measures had been increased yet [again —] only clear plastic bags allowed o[n ...] planes, no liquids – the list of restricti[ons was] huge. " Dude", she said " This is [such a] Crazy world now – SUCH a Crazy Wor[ld!"] I couldn't agree more. September 1[1 ...]

CRAZY WORLD

Monday

The alarm sounds an early start to my Monday morning. My feet swing out of bed and hit the floor. I sit for a minute and wonder to myself, "Why is it that the Monday morning alarm is so loud? I'm sure it isn't that loud every other morning." And so my day starts.

My Monday could be filled with one or more large events. I might be preparing for a birthday celebration. I might be starting a new phase in my job. Or I might be attending one of many school events with my children. A number of those things do seem worthy to be captured in photographs and told as a story on a scrapbook page. However, when we look behind those large events, when we really look at the details, we see the finer points of life. It is those finer points that really tell the story of who we are.

Look around and notice the everyday items. Notice the routines that we all do without thinking or really hear the conversations that might be different by tomorrow. Our children grow up. Pets come and go. Situations and jobs change. People move on. Everyday favorite items in our home are replaced. These details of our lives are an integral part of the way we live every single day and we need to recognize them in our artwork.

TUESDAY

WEDNESDAY

THURSDAY

FRIDAY

SATURDAY

SUNDAY

9

Record a Daily Diary

Consider noting what happens each day in a diary-style format. Instead of concentrating on the actual events, write down funny things that were said and situations that made you smile or laugh during the day. Keep a notepad sitting on the kitchen counter, in your car or perhaps at your workplace for just one day. Cut your day into the smallest details and note those moments. Soon you will have a notepad full of small details that when put into the big picture will show a truer story of you.

I don't think many people have taken a photo of the last banana in the fruit bowl and immortalized it on a scrapbook page. I think I am fairly unique in that aspect, but when you look at the page you can see it is more than a page about a banana. It is a page about a typical conversation that took place one day in our kitchen. It incorporates both the personalities of my husband and myself, and reveals an aspect of our relationship with each other. The journaling contains details of other things currently in our home, such as a toddler and her behavior, school-age children and the fact that I make their lunches daily. It finishes with a joke about my culinary skills or lack thereof.

At first glance it is a layout about a banana. But on closer inspection you can see more. The information revealed about my home with this one page is a testament to the fact that we all need to record the funny conversations and the little things every once in a while. Find a notepad and place it somewhere handy to write down those little conversations and details in your day. You might be surprised at the inspiration those details can provide.

The Last Banana

JUST WHAT WILL BECOME OF THIS LAST SAD BANANA?

THE LAST Banana...

LEFT UNTIL THE SPOTS TAKE OVER AND BEING THROWN AWAY. BANANA MUFFINS (OK SO NOT LIKELY)

BEING PUT IN A LUNCH BOX ONLY TO BE RETURNED IN A WORSE STATE (AND ULTIMATELY BEING THROWN AWAY).

BEING GRABBED BY THE TODDLER-MONSTER, PARTIALLY EATEN AND THE REMAINDER SMASHED AROUND THE PLACE.

JUST SOME OF THE THINGS PAUL & I CAME UP WITH,

IN A TOTALLY RANDOM BUT AWESOMELY FUNNY CONVERSATION WE HAD TODAY.

July '06

TUESDAY

WEDNESDAY

THURSDAY

FRIDAY

SATURDAY

SUNDAY

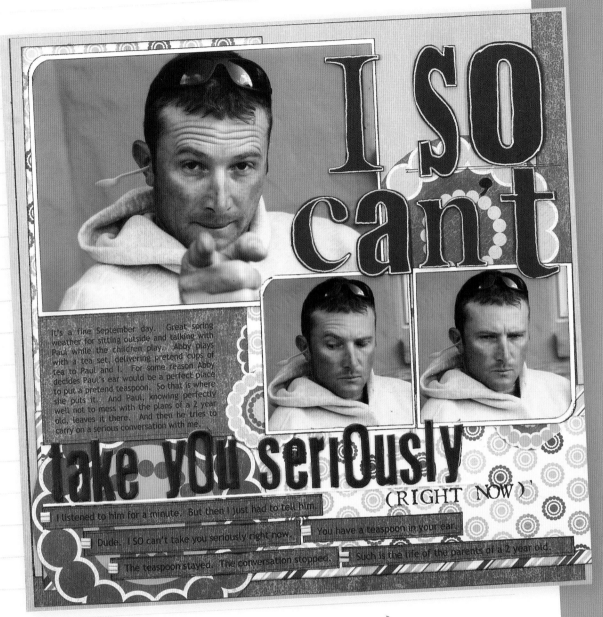

I So Can't Take You Seriously (Right Now)

Parenting a toddler is a wild ride. It's demanding, challenging and some days it has me pulling my hair out. Mostly though, it is rewarding. I could write typical journaling to go with an angelic picture of my daughter, but I chose to capture these times in a different way. There is no picture of an angelic child on this page. Instead, there is a series of photos of my husband with a toy teaspoon in his ear, and journaling that explains who put it there. It is a perfect illustration to give the reader a feeling for Abby's personality, and also communicate an understanding of what it is like to live in a home with a two-year-old.

Monday Morning Alarm

The noise of the morning alarm has to be one of the sounds I dread most. I never quite get used to being abruptly awoken in the morning. I admit I do my fair share of complaining about getting out of bed. Everyone hears about it. It's one of those things that will be embedded in my mind and my children's minds for years to come. I'm sure alarm clocks won't always look like this, and one day my children will relate to my morning angst. I see that as a perfectly valid reason to create artwork.

WHY

Is the MONDAY MORNING alarm so LOUD?

(I swear it's not that loud on the other days of the week)

not my daughter

"Girls are so stubborn – wait til she starts to dress herself".

"Aha", I said, nodding.   Not my daughter, I thought.

"Girls are different – you wait til she starts to refuse certain clothes".

"Aha", I said, nodding. "Not my daughter", I thought.

Not My Daughter

Initially I didn't think having a daughter was so different from having two sons. I'll never forget one of my friends warning me it would all change once Abby could open her own drawers and take out her own clothes. I stood and laughed along with the conversation, but in the back of my mind I thought to myself, "Not my daughter." Then the day came when Abby could open her own drawers and get out her own clothes. She never looked back. My daughter developed a stubbornness to match all the stories I'd been told. I could tell similar stories to warn new mums of baby girls, but instead I'll record the evidence and put it on a page to capture a phase that will quickly pass.

TUESDAY

WEDNESDAY

THURSDAY

FRIDAY

SATURDAY

SUNDAY

13

Things I Would Miss

Some things become such a constant in our lives that we don't realize we will miss them until they are gone. Each day arrives and we go about our daily business with these **things** being a regular part of life. Some are physical items, some are environmental factors beyond our control and some are behaviors of the people around us that will change as we each move onto the next phase or stage in our lives.

Take time to think about some of those constants. Write down the small, seemingly unimportant events that happen every day. These things often provide the structure of our day-to-day living. They are the why, where and what of our families and relationships. These little things range from the children watching TV (and what they are watching), to our pet's favorite place to lie in the sun, to the routines when our significant other comes home from work or play.

The page "Daddy's Home!" captures several of those constants. The journaling talks of the sound of the car coming down the road at the end of the day. Goodness knows, as the mother of three young children, there is nothing like the relief I feel as I hear that sound, knowing help is on the way! The pictures show two important things—the children waving at Daddy as he arrives home and Paul driving up the driveway. I know we won't have that same vehicle forever, and in decades to come we will no doubt laugh at it! I also know for sure that the time my children will want to wave at their daddy is temporary.

Daddy's Home!

Monday

TUESDAY

WEDNESDAY

THURSDAY

FRIDAY

SATURDAY

SUNDAY

WHAT IS THAT SOUND?

daddy's home

love

For as long as it has been that Paul and I have lived in the same home, I have sub-consciously listened, and found comfort in, the sound of him driving down the road to turn in the driveway at the end of the day.

We have been together for over 15 years now, and he has owned many vehicles in that time. From the little red ute he owned that was extremely distinctive, to the white Pajero that I could hardly hear. Each has sounded differently, but in my mind I can still hear that sound of him changing down through the gears as he slows for home.

Now we have children and they have become tuned to that same sound. They love the sound of daddy driving down the road to come home at the end of the day.

It is one of those things that we hear everyday, so we don't really notice how much we rely on it for comfort. Seeing the kids at the window the other day bought it home for me though. We all love the sound of daddy driving down the road at the end of the day.

YAY!

As a 3 year old you used to get up early each morning. You were good about getting out of bed and quietly going and turning the TV on and settling down.

I would find you each morning sitting, fixated with Thomas the Tank Engine on the TV screen.

As you got older you started to sleep in.

YOU DIDN'T WATCH THOMAS ANYMORE.

Just the other day you got up early. You came through and switched on the TV and settled down. I walked through and saw Thomas on TV. I gave you a quick kiss Good Morning and said "Oh look, it's Thomas, you used to love Thomas!" I walked away from you with a warm glow of "remember when".

"I don't like Thomas anymore" you said as you clicked the TV remote.
I LOVE THIS POKEMON STUFF!

Talk about stop a mother in her tracks. I guess I just wasn't ready for that one.

You Used to Love Thomas

In the world of a preschooler, favorite friends, toys, games, and even programs they watch on TV are all reflections of their true personality. When Braden was a preschooler, I could guarantee that he would always be out of bed before us, and that he would always turn on the TV and watch **Thomas the Tank Engine** while he waited for us to greet him for the morning. Snuggling down on the couch watching Thomas became something of a morning ritual with my little man.

It wasn't until I saw **Thomas** on TV again recently that I realized we had stopped that small ritual. It was something so constant in our daily routine, yet I didn't realize it had become an important part of my day until it was gone. Creating this layout about Braden will help me remember those preschool days with him, and the fleeting things that made those days special.

Note to Self
Evana Willis

Evana's layout features her son, Liam, and his current habit of sleeping in her bed when Daddy is away from home. It is a somewhat ironic, comical look at something that happens often, and she admits it makes her night's sleep less than perfect! The gorgeous part about this layout is the hidden sentiment. Although Liam's habit of sleeping in her bed can be annoying, one day it won't happen anymore. It seems that all too sudden our children stop showing us they need us, and we feel they are growing way too fast. Evana has collected her thoughts about this experience perfectly. There is nothing wrong with scrapping these small moments that annoy us, because despite our feelings at the time, often we miss these things when they are gone.

NOTE TO SELF

When Daddy is away on business, **NEVER EVER EVER** let my 6 year old son sleep in my bed! For some reason this little guy thinks that when Daddy is away he has an open pass to fill the other side of the bed. **LET ME SAY THAT THIS IS JUST NOT SO!** I mean don't get me wrong...I love his cuddles & I love being close to him...BUT HOLY MOLY GUACAMOLE!!! That little guy can wriggly & kick like crazy. The bed is a king-size but he can still dominate it. Being heavily pregnant, I was so darn conscious of him kicking me that I had to turn my back to him. Never the less, he got closer, & closer, & closer to me & I got closer & closer to the edge. I felt like the little teddy bear in that nursery rhyme. You know the little one that said "Roll over, Roll over" except I was the one that fell off! Needless to say... I have learnt my lesson.

serene relaxed safe

serene relaxed safe const

you should be here

Monday

TUESDAY

WEDNESDAY

THURSDAY

FRIDAY

SATURDAY

SUNDAY

Lesson 2

Things I Would Miss

Today, you caught one of the rainbow prisms that come in through the beveled cut glass windows in our home. It's not every day that we get to see the glass catch the sun to create little rainbows throughout the house – you have to be up early and the sun has to be at just the right angle in the sky. In the 20 years that we have lived here, all of our children have tried to catch the rainbows. They'd climb onto the back of the couch to catch one on their tummy, or sit on the floor to see one rest upon their legs, appearing to turn them striped with purple, yellow, pink, and blue paint. There always seems to be something magical about a rainbow, but it's an extra special day when you can catch one for your very own.

Catching Rainbows
Linda Albrecht

During the twenty years that Linda has lived in the same home, she has noticed the rainbows that reflect in through the windows. They only cast themselves across the floor when the light and position of the sun are perfect, so they don't happen all the time. But they do happen enough to have become a familiarity in her home. As long as Linda can remember, her children have tried to catch these rainbows. They have played games catching them on their tummies or legs, or in their hands. It is an example of one of those common activities that we take for granted because we see it happen so often. Linda has noticed as her children get older, catching rainbows isn't as desirable anymore. So she was grateful to take this picture of her son, on one of the rare moments he was up early enough and the sun was at the right angle in the sky.

Daily Frustrations

Whatever our circumstances, we all have **stuff** that makes our skin crawl. This stuff might be things we hate to do, things that bug us endlessly or things we know we have to deal with, but we'd rather not. Often these things won't be around forever. We might leave the job that annoys us. The children, grandchildren or pets will grow older and their habits will change. Our teenager will stop breaking house rules and move away from home. We might buy a new appliance or car or home and the things about the old ones that annoyed us will soon be forgotten. Our family and friends now hear us refer to these annoyances constantly but twenty years from now, when situations have changed, it'll be interesting to remember some of them, to look back and laugh.

Although some of the situations might be negative, the pages we create don't have to be. For example, on the layout "Things That Make Me Go Grrr" each one of the items included annoys me incredibly. I constantly voice my irritation to my husband and children, usually to no avail. I listed some of these things and took pictures of a few of them. They frustrate me and make life difficult at the moment. But I know it won't always be that way. I love that I have this layout in my album. It gives a clever insight into my personality, the things that are important, and the things that are certainly not important in my day.

Things That Make Me Go Grrr

THINGS

That make me go grrr

Empty Chocolate Wrappers. Avocado. Cleaning the fish tank. Running out of milk. The cold. Broccoli. Full Rubbish bins. Spiders on my clothesline. 2 T.V.s and the radio on at once. Toys left outside. A messy lounge. CDs not put back in their cases. Drivers that don't indicate. An empty gas tank. Items too high on the shelf at the supermarket. Folding washing. Winter time. Email not working. Bad manners. Peeling potatoes. Hay fever season. The washing machine eating socks. Headaches. Holes in my favourite jeans.

Monday
TUESDAY
WEDNESDAY
THURSDAY
FRIDAY
SATURDAY
SUNDAY

Diva Days

The Terrible Twos—a glorious time of life, where a child starts to learn she does have a mind of her own and begins to exercise her rights by refusing to cooperate. As Abby approached the twos and her behavior started to change, I asked the mums around me many questions about what to expect. They all remember the Terrible Twos, but looking back through their photos they all have smiling pictures of their **saintly** child. The photos contradict the times they really remember. I needed to record more than this. Although most of our days are wonderful, Abby at two is not always an angelic child. I needed to record the true essence of two, in all its finger pointing, high-pitched squealing, refusing to cooperate real life beauty. Because this is just a phase. And it shall pass. I repeat to myself: it shall pass.

Trivial
Evana Willis

It is easy to laugh when we read the journaling in Evana's layout. We may not all share what she calls her "non-negotiable obsession," but most of us can relate to it one way or another. Evana admits she has asked her husband and children many times to help her keep that part of her home clean, and it seems she is not listened to. Something that endlessly irritates her has been turned into a layout that captures both her frustrations and her sense of humor.

Who, Me?
Courtney Walsh

It seems the annoying actions of toddlers is a worldwide theme. Courtney explained that the afternoon she took this photo of her son it was a true trial to keep herself calm. Ethan had tested her patience by, among other things, flushing an entire roll of toilet paper and smashing a light bulb. Courtney wrote the journaling in a witty tone from her son's point of view. It turned a frustrating afternoon into an event that Courtney can look at a little more light-heartedly. While it certainly wasn't funny at the time, it is a perfect example of capturing the personality of someone important to us in a layout.

Monday

TUESDAY

WEDNESDAY

THURSDAY

FRIDAY

SATURDAY

SUNDAY

The Essential Me

It is Tuesday afternoon and I'm relaxing in the lounge with a hot drink and a chocolate. It's only taken me thirty years to realize I occasionally need to take time out for myself. Because when it comes down to it, I need to understand that no one is more important to my life than me. None of the people in my life, my family especially, would exist in the capacity they do were I not to say, act and care the way I do. It is the same for all of us. Whether we have children or not, whether we have an away-from-home job or not, whether we spend a lot of time with friends or not, we all have an essential framework of personality traits. And these traits have an influence on the structuring and forming of the people around us, just as others' personality traits have structured and formed us.

From the perspective of friends and family, it would be interesting to know some of the little things about us that have affected them. I'm sure my children's future partners might like to know why my children have a tendency to neglect the cleaning of their cars or avoid avocados. Or perhaps my children will be the opposite of me, but in the scheme of things it does matter. I know there are a few things I do, or avoid doing, that I'd love to know whether I inherited from someone. I'd love to hear the personal stories of days gone past that might have ultimately contributed to the way I am today. Sharing those personality traits, those innermost thoughts, hopes and fears isn't just all about you—it's about sharing yourself with others.

MONDAY

Tuesday

WEDNESDAY

THURSDAY

FRIDAY

SATURDAY

SUNDAY

Why Do You Do That?

We all have them. We all have those little habits, quirks and unchangeable personality traits. I've laughed as I watched my son cutting paper, concentrating so hard that his jaw opens and shuts with each stroke of the scissors. If I were to ask him why he does it, he would have no idea. He just knows that cutting the paper is so much harder without those actions.

Because we are usually unaware of our own quirks, they probably will not be the subject of our personal layouts. Yet many of these mannerisms and actions will be what others will remember about us, so that in itself warrants recognizing.

One of the clues to discovering these little aspects of our personality is when someone asks, "Why do you do that? What makes you do that in that way?" These questions provide a great prompt that can lead to a very cool page. Take a look at your own quirks; document those behaviors, and know they are the little things friends and family will remember about you.

The lightbulb moment for me came during a shopping trip with my husband. The kids needed clothes, as did I. I'm a quick shopper. I walk through the aisles, casually stopping to look at an item that catches my eye. If I really like something, I give it the **scrunch test**. I grab the lower edge of the clothing item and scrunch the material hard in my hands. Paul says to me, "Why do you do that? Why do you need to do that?" So I educated him on the fine art of scrunch testing. If the wrinkles don't fall out when I take my hand away, I don't buy the item. I do not iron. My mother did not iron. I grew up in a "thou shall not need to iron" environment. I see no need to change that. When the clothing passes the scrunch test, the shopping trip is complete. I come away with the day's shopping and an idea for a page about yet another personal character trait. The page I created from this revelation not only captured a habit my husband and children have seen me do for years but also captured the reasoning behind it. It includes details about the way I was bought up. Because I don't own an iron, the scrunch test is a vital part of all clothing purchases. That in itself is something future readers of my scrapbooks will value learning about me.

Scrunch Test

the scrunch test

Step 1. Decide on the garment you might like to purchase.

Step 2. Take the edge of the clothing in your hand

Step 3: Scrunch fabric.

Step 4: Take hand away to reveal fabric.

Step5: Assess the crinkle-factor.

If the fabric is highly crinkled it is possible that this piece of clothing may need to be ironed after washing.

Do not buy item of clothing.

I do not iron. My mother did not iron. I grew up in a "thou shalt not need to iron" environment. I see no need to change that.

The scrunch test prevails.

MONDAY

TUESDAY

WEDNESDAY

THURSDAY

FRIDAY

SATURDAY

SUNDAY

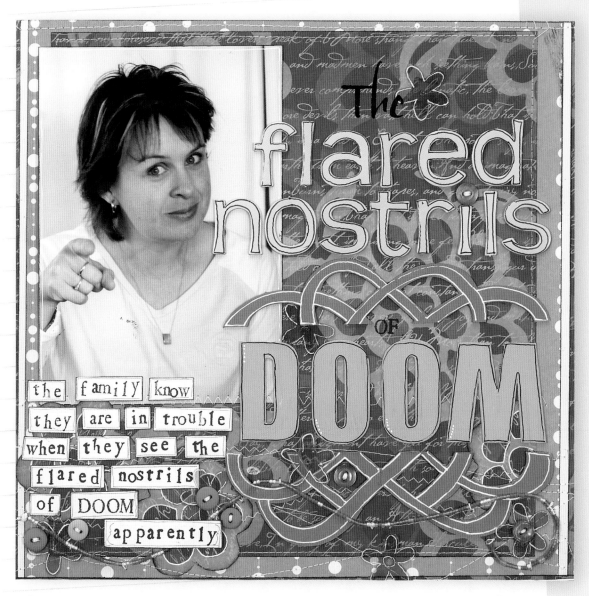

The flared nostrils OF DOOM

the family know they are in trouble when they see the flared nostrils of DOOM apparently

Flared Nostrils of DOOM

I had no idea I did it. Apparently I flare my nostrils when I am trying to get a point across in conversation. It was only recently pointed out to me. In fact, I think it was pointed out by my husband in an effort to make me laugh during one of **those** very conversations when I was trying to get my point across. He called them "The Flared Nostrils of Doom." I admit I stopped mid-sentence and laughed. The kids have not let the teasing stop, especially when I am fully involved in lecturing them about something important. I'm sure this one is going down in the history books of the Howard home.

The Great Shoe Debate
Lisa VanderVeen

We all have those little habits that drive the others in our home crazy. For Lisa it's leaving her shoes all around the house. It annoys her husband to no end, yet it is was something Lisa hadn't even realized she did. Although Lisa fully intends to put her shoes upstairs, at some point she ends up kicking them off. Lisa now realizes that she has this habit, but it did take her husband pointing it out several times before she really got it.

The Order of the Stuff on the Sandwich

Paul is so good about making his lunch every morning before he goes to work. It is something I have seen him do for years. I've watched him place the meat, then the sauce, then the cheese, tomato, capsicum (bell pepper) and finish with the salad greens. I have also watched him go into a virtual state of panic if one of his ingredients is missing. It's even more fun if I hide one of the ingredients, like I did on this day. Paul denies that he is so strict about the order of the ingredients on the sandwich. I just know it is something I have witnessed every single morning for the past fifteen years and it has always been the same. It's fun to have both the everyday event and the personality trait that it reveals documented on my page.

27

MONDAY

Tuesday

WEDNESDAY

THURSDAY

FRIDAY

SATURDAY

SUNDAY

Our Innermost Thoughts

Whether we are stay-at-home mothers, working mothers, grandmothers, footloose and single or from any other walk of life, in this day and age most of us would describe ourselves as being busy. It's usually the answer I give when anyone asks how I'm doing. However, despite how hectic our lives seem to be, there are various moments throughout our day when we are alone, if only for a few moments. It's those moments when we can take time to think, collect our thoughts and maybe even write those thoughts down. These little glimpses into our minds are excellent representations of our day-to-day living.

A perfect example of how I put my thoughts onto paper without even realizing it came in the form of an e-mail I sent to a friend one night. The e-mail consisted of things I had chatted about during the day, topics we had shared through previous e-mails, situations I was currently involved in and ended with my hopes for the coming day. I formulated the e-mail as a prayer, pressed "send," turned off the computer and went to bed.

When I got up the next morning, my friend had e-mailed me back. She told me I was nuts, but also wished me the best for all the things I wanted to happen in the new day. As I re-read what I had written and was reminded of the situations from the day before, I saw that I had the perfect journaling for a layout. What truer reflection of my own thoughts than something I had spontaneously written.

Often the stories that best reflect us in our layouts are not the obvious ones. They are the e-mails we write. They are the random thoughts that come to mind as we go about our day. They are the conversations we have with others. Use a notepad to write down some of these thoughts, or take a look at the e-mails you have written. Using this writing as journaling, you'll be surprised how much of your inner self can be encapsulated in a layout.

Prayer

PRAYER

Dear Lord we thank you for this day

and for the things it may bring us.

We thank you for the chocolate

and for the 2lbs it has bought

us in the   last 2 weeks,

we know there are people out there less

fortunate as us, as we remind our kids everyday

if they dont eat all their meal

we thank you for the family and friends

you have graced us with.

We pray to you that tomorrow treat us kindly,

may the sun shine, may peace

enlighten the hearts

of friends and family

and may Scenic Route have

emailed me by the morning.

Amen.

July '06

MONDAY

TUESDAY

WEDNESDAY

THURSDAY

FRIDAY

SATURDAY

SUNDAY

BUT... IT WAS THE PLAN

For as long as I can remember, I have had a passion for the written word. In high school, I wrote poetry and short stories and several of them won me major contests. It was my dream to become a journalist. More than that, it was my PLAN. I could envision myself traveling the world for famous newspapers and magazines, and writing... In fact, it became such a big part of who I was and who I wanted to be that when I had my grad ring created, I had it engraved with "journalism" on its side, along with a typewriter and quill. There it was, engraved, forever... no turning back, now. I entered college, majoring in translation, learning German and the plan was that after 2 years, I was going to enter University in journalism. It was all decided... down to which university I would attend.

But the plan went out the window.
I had to quit my first semester in college to take care of my dying mother. I went back in January, only to quit, once again... this time after learning I was expecting. But... this was NOT the plan!!! I had never planned to be orphaned and get pregnant at 17. I hadn't planned that I'd have to support a family and therefore that my Plan A, my journalism studies, could not happen.

It's 13 years later. I am 30 now. I'm so glad that my original plan never came true. I would not be who and where I am today if it had. By age 25, I had three children. I have been in scrapbooking, which serves as an outlet for my urge to write, to create, to meet people, to travel. Although I got a diploma in floral design from a professional school. But this time, it's not set in stone, not engraved anywhere. I have faith in life. I am happy with what I've done so far... life will guide me...
Maybe THAT was the plan.

The Plan
Caro Huot

Sometimes our innermost thoughts are not just from a single moment or a single day. They might be a series of thoughts that have grouped themselves in our mind for so long that they become part of our being—the often unspoken or unwritten hopes or expectations we have for ourself. Caro's layout perfectly conveys her thoughts from teenage years. The page features a close-up photo of her graduation ring and its engraving. Her journaling not only explains the engraving on the ring, for anyone who inherits it in the future, but also provides Caro with a sense of closure by admitting her thoughts **out loud** on a layout.

Distracted by the Train

My love for trains is something no one really knows about. I haven't pursued **train spotting** or pushed myself to find out more about them. It's a fascination I hadn't really even admitted to myself, until I nearly got into a car accident due to being distracted while I strained to see a train going past. When I told a friend about how close I came to hitting the car in front of me, she was surprised at what had distracted me. "I had no idea you loved trains!" My husband's reaction was the same. At that point it occurred to me that this was a facet of my personality I hadn't really shared. What more fun way to portray it than in a layout that describes a very close incident that almost proved to everyone just how much I do love trains.

I love trains. I will go out of my way to make sure I am next to the railway station when I know one is due to pass by. When we see a train I will drive to the nearest rail crossing so I can sit and watch it racing past as the bells go DING DING DING and the red lights flash.

Not many people know this about me. Yesterday I was on my way to buy some groceries. I had to go over a rail bridge just before the store. There was a train going under the bridge as I went over. I strained to see the train whilst trying to concentrate on the car in front and the driveway to the store. I obviously lost concentration for just a minute. I was *this close* to hitting that car in front.

I kind of had a moment right there. One where I imagined filling out the insurance forms. Reason for accident? I was distracted by a train...

MONDAY
Tuesday
WEDNESDAY
THURSDAY
FRIDAY
SATURDAY
SUNDAY

Lesson 2

Our Innermost Thoughts

THAT'S a STrong wiND TODAY.
THE washing SHOULD Dry WELL.
i WON'T HAVE TO USE THE Dryer.
i might even go CHANGE SOME BEDS.
THE SOCKS are in Pairs aND NONE are missing.

i HATE Pairing SOCKS.

ESPECIALLY OUT OF THE Dryer.
THEY STICK TO EVERYTHING WITH THAT STATIC ELECTRICITY.
i NEED TO Pay THAT POWEr BILL iN THE
Drawer. i MUST DO THAT,
maybe once i'm FINISHED WITH

THIS washing

i CAN Hear a SKYLARK.
i LOVE THAT SOUND.
IT'S a summer is coming SOUND.
i woNDer
WHEN PAUL WILL PLANT SOME summer vegies.
THE TOMATOES WENT WELL
LAST year.
i COULD EVEN BOTTLE SOME sauce THIS year.

PIZZa sauce

i NEED TO THiNK OF SOMETHING
TO MAKE FOR DINNEr.
i THiNK i HAVE SOME LEFTOVER
sausages iN THE FRIDGE.
aBBY WON'T EAT THEM THOUGH,
SHE is iS SO Picky.
i DON'T remember THE BOYS
BEiNG SO Picky aT THIS age.
maybe THEY Were
THAT Picky.
i woNDer HOW THE
BOYS are DOiNG aT
SCHOOL TODAY.
IT'S quite warm aND i
DiDN'T PUT SUNBLOCK
ON THEM.
IT'D BE a great Day TO

HANG OUT

No

RANDOM THOUGHTS

2008

the WASHING

Hang Out the Washing

Time when I am alone and free to think is something I treasure. Three young children make for a busy and noisy home. I find my thoughts wander while doing housework, walking the children to and from school or driving places. It wasn't until I was hanging out the washing one day, in one of those quiet momentary personal retreats, that I realized what random chains of thought sometimes go through my mind. It was fun to come inside and write them down to include in a layout. Reading this journaling is a little glimpse into my thought patterns for the day.

Joking with Friends

We all have funny little things we do. Usually the people around us pick up on these things. Now and then they become topics of conversation or friendly ridicule. For example, my friends and family know I hate avocados with a passion. They joke about it with me. I make fun of it, too. I encounter the same amount of ridicule about other little idiosyncrasies. And I give as much back as I receive.

It is a morning routine for me to run the dishwasher right after I clean up the kitchen following breakfast. If I have visitors, the kettle is set to boil, cups of coffee are made and tempting chocolate muffins or cookies are served. Something else that I can count on, when friends join me for tea, is the ridicule that I will receive about my dishwasher quirk. They **know** I am obsessive about getting the clean dishes put away before dirtying more dishes. It's been the subject of much laughter around the kitchen table over morning tea. I know it is one of my personal quirks, and I enjoy the friendly conversation about it.

I'm sure it has been the same through the generations. I'm sure my mum and my grandmother had the same relationship with their friends, and I'm sure the same kind of joking and friendly ridicule took place. I wish I had insight into some of those things. Our quirks paint a picture of our personality in a way that we could never describe ourselves. Making an effort to write down some of these situations and create a page based around them is a perfect way to share the details of who you are.

Lesson 3

Dishwasher 101

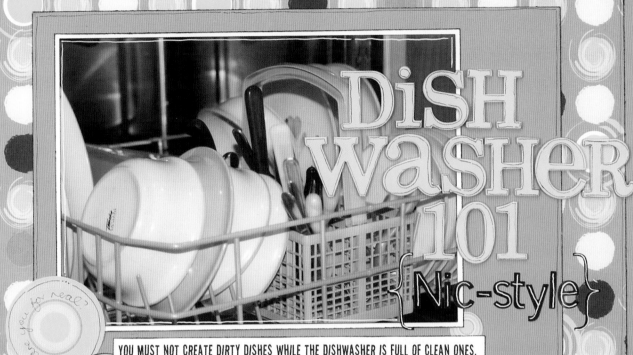

DiSH WaSHER 101
{Nic-style}

YOU MUST NOT CREATE DIRTY DISHES WHILE THE DISHWASHER IS FULL OF CLEAN ONES.

IF YOU FORGET TO EMPTY DISHWASHER AND YOU CREATE DIRTY DISHES, YOU MUST GO INTO HOWARD DISHWASHER SAFETY MODE TO FIX THE SITUATION.

EMPTY THE DISHWASHER BUT DO NOT PLACE ANY CLEAN DISHES ON THE BENCH NEXT TO A DIRTY ONE,

THEY MUST GO DIRECTLY TO THEIR CORRECT PLACES, DO NOT PASS GO, DO NOT COLLECT $200.

EMERGENCY WILL BE AVERTED IF YOU DO THIS NOW.

TOTALLY. YES SERIOUSLY I MEAN IT ...

are you for real?
I really mean it?
do you not seriously?
YES.

MONDAY
Tuesday
WEDNESDAY
THURSDAY
FRIDAY
SATURDAY
SUNDAY

(sidebar journaling, rotated text:)
...on't wash my car (often). Occasionally the next-door neighbour gets $5.00 for washing it. This would only be once or twice a year, ...haps. My friends laugh. I am ridiculed. It is all in fun though. Although recently someone found moss growing on my car. This would only be once or twice a year, perhaps. My friends laugh. I am ridiculed. It is all in fun though. Lucky for me it still drives to school to drop off the kids. ...e teasing got a little stronger then. Okay already. My car grows moss. Lucky for me it still goes at the speed of other motorists. ...till takes me where I want to go and surprisingly, even though it is dirty and grows moss, it still goes at the speed of other motorists. ...ade sure when I bought the car that it was the version that would do all these things whether it was dirty or not :o) SEPT '06

MY CAR GROWS **moss**

It still gets me places...

My Car Grows Moss

I've seen people washing their cars and I know I probably need to do it more often. I never seem to find the time. I admit my car often goes unwashed for long periods. My friends and family love to write messages in the dust on my car and make fun of the fact that it is no longer blue, but a dusty shade of earth. And that is okay by me. I guess the crunch came, though, when someone spotted moss growing on it. I received a barrage of teasing e-mails over that one. I replied with a friendly banter about how my car goes the same speed and still gets me places whether it grows moss or not. I can just imagine the children saying to their children when they grow up, "When I was a kid, my mother drove a car that grew moss!" Yep. Sure did. And I have the page to prove it.

Avocado

Avocado makes me shudder. Who knew that a food could make me shudder? It's hard for me to imagine and I'm sure that it's hard for those around me to understand. It's also the perfect personal quirk for my friends and family to ridicule. I don't mind. I will never forget the time I had friends over for dinner and afterward had a sink full of dishes to wash. I saw a piece of avocado on a plate in the water and I had to let the dishwater go and run clean water. I admit this is crazy. It's a weird obsession, but at least my children know what they are dealing with. Luckily I have a layout to explain my avocado quirk.

don't make me

Go ahead. Make fun of me.

Make fun of the fact that I cannot touch avocado.

I cannot even bear the thought of touching it.

just this ONE funny habit...

Don't use a knife that has cut an avocado on my food.

The image of actually eating it makes me gag.

If it gets in the dishwater, I have to run a new sink full.

touch AVOCADO

PLEASE. Don't make me touch it.

Small Elephant

Can anybody else say they can fit their children inside their mailbox? Hands up. No? I can. The downside to marrying someone in the construction industry is that we move often. We build homes and we sell them. It's not often that we are in a home for more than about a year. The upside to marrying someone in the construction industry is that Paul always builds me the best mailboxes. I have found that, as scrapbooking has played a larger part in my life, my mailboxes have gotten larger. As my neighbor said, when she saw our latest mailbox, "You could fit a small elephant in there!" It's important, right? You must have a large mailbox to fit those 12" x 12" boxes completely inside. We don't want them getting wet.

"You could fit a SMALL eLepHanT" in that mailbox.

As quoted by my neighbour...

More proof that a scrapper lives here.

MONDAY
TUESDAY
WEDNESDAY
THURSDAY
FRIDAY
SATURDAY
SUNDAY

Wednesday

MONDAY

TUESDAY

Wednesday

THURSDAY

FRIDAY

SATURDAY

SUNDAY

Wednesday arrives and it is cold. I'm curled up by the fireplace, knowing I have errands to run and jobs to do, but it's hard to move away. I have always loved to sit in front of the fireplace, ever since I was a little girl.

Our days are full of subtle reminiscing. Our children ask questions about when we were little or, even without them asking, we offer the information. I often hear myself saying, "I can't believe we used to...." or "How did we do without...?" Lately, with the speed that technology is developing, we say it more and more often.

These conversations are perfect information to turn into scrapbook pages. Your experiences today are forming a history future generations will love and value hearing about. I know I find some of the tales unbelievable that my dad told me from forty years ago. I certainly wish he had the photos and anecdotes in scrapbooks to show me. It encourages me to keep my mind open, to hear the stories those around me are telling, and to get them into scrapbook pages whenever possible.

Do You Remember When?

On the way home the other day, my husband and I drove by a boy riding his bike on the sidewalk—head down, legs pumping, the back of his jacket flapping behind him in the wind. As we passed by, he gave up his race, stopped peddling and coasted down the hill.

Seeing that boy indulge in a **race** with our car instantly took me back twenty-five years. The conversation that followed consisted of "Do you remember when?" and talk of favorite toys and friends. And of course I talked about my old bike that probably didn't look quite like that one, but similar. As we reminisced about these things, we wondered what happened to some of our favorite toys and bikes, and at what point it became uncool to race cars and have tassels on the handlebars. I spoke of the basket and pretty tassels that I had on my bike when I was a kid. Paul spoke of racing along the sidewalk trying to beat the cars that passed by, just like the little boy we'd seen earlier.

"Do you remember when?" Those four words are magical. They indicate that we are remembering something that is gone, something that usually won't come back, and all we have are the images and stories in our mind. Although these stories still seem fresh in our memory, they are probably amusing to our children. Those little gems are perfect subject matter for layouts. If you don't have photos, try asking friends or relatives. They may have just the right photo to go with your story, so you can get the memory on paper.

We Were So Cool

Driving down the road the other day Paul & I passed by a kid riding his bike. As he saw us approach he put his head down and pedalled as fast as he could. He gave up his race as we passed

Do you remember doing that when you were little?

Yea, I said. We were so cool.

Did you have one of those cool chopper bikes with the big orange triangle flag off the back?

Yep, I said, my brother had a bike called a tomahawk.
It was state of the art skid-on-the-gravel-driveway material

it was SO cool

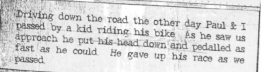

SO COOL

Nic & Shane 1977

MONDAY

TUESDAY

Wednesday

THURSDAY

FRIDAY

SATURDAY

SUNDAY

Growing Up in New Zealand: I'm talking about hide and seek/spotlight in the backyard late into the summer evenings at Christmas time. The corner dairy, hopscotch, four square, go carts, non-stop cricket and inviting everyone on your street to join in, skipping, handstands, elastics, bullrush, ,slip'n'slides, the trampoline with water on it (or a sprinkler under it), jumping in puddles with gumboots on, mud pies and building dams in the gutter. The smell of the sun and fresh cut grass on a Sunday. "Big bubbles no troubles" with Hubba Bubba bubble gum. A topsy. Mr Whippy cones on a warm summer night after you've chased him round the block. 20 cents worth of mixed lollies lasted a week and pretending to smoke "fags" (the lollies) was really cool! A dollars worth of chips from the take-away fed two people. Watching Saturday morning cartoons: 'The Smurfs', 'AstroBoy', 'He-man', 'Captain Caveman', 'Teenage Mutant Ninja Turtles', 'Jem' (trulyoutrageous!!), Sigmund and the Sea Monsters and 'Heeeey heeeeey heeeeeeeey it's faaaaaaat Albert'. Or staying up late being amazed when you watched TV right up until the 'Goodnight Kiwi! 'When After School with Jason Gunn & Thingie had a cult following and What Now was on Saturday mornings! When around the corner seemed a long way, and going into town seemed like going somewhere. A million mozzie bites, building huts out on the farm and catching tadpoles in horse troughs. Going down to the school swimming pool when you didn't have a key and your friends let you in, drawing all over the road and driveway with chalk. Climbing trees and building huts out of every sheet your mum had in the cupboard. When writing 'I love....? on your pencil case, really did mean it was true love. Laughing so hard that your stomach hurt. Pitching the tent in the back/front yard (and never being able to find all the pegs). Singing into your hairbrush in front of the mirror, making mix tapes off the radio, and becoming frustrated when the DJ talked too much over the start of the song. Eating raw jelly and raro, and sucking on a popsicle, or a T-T-Two... You knew everyone in your street - and so did your parents! It wasn't odd to have two or three "best friends" and you would ask them by sending a note asking them to be your best friend. It was magic when dad would "remove" his thumb. When it was considered a great privilege to be taken out to dinner at the local Cobb'n'Co with your family. Where bluelight discos were the equivalent to a Rave, and asking a boy out meant writing a 'polite' note getting them to tick 'yes' or 'no'. Going to the beach and catching a wave was a dream come true. Boogie boarding in the whitewash made you the next Kelly Slater.

it's the journey not the destination

this is one incredible adventure

this is one incredible adventure

home

Home

I received an e-mail the other day; it was one of those e-mails that makes the rounds. Kinda funny, a little humorous…it made me smile. I don't often read them, but this one caught my eye— **You know you grew up in New Zealand when**. I read the first few lines and smiled a little. I read more and laughed a little. I read even more and called my husband over to read with me. "Do you remember this stuff?" I found myself saying. Although I didn't have a picture that came from the times of my life reflected in the journaling, I had a current photo of my children that was perfect. I grew up with these things, and they will grow up with many of them too.

Wow, Really?

The idea for this page came from a casual conversation with my children about phones and phone numbers. I mentioned to them that my first phone number was only three digits. Their little jaws dropped. "No way!!! Wow, really?" I guess, although it is fresh in my mind, in their world of nine-digit phone numbers they find it unbelievable. As we continued to talk, it occurred to me that they had never been exposed to a world where you had to sit in one place to have a phone conversation with the handset joined to the phone. At that point it became clear that I needed to scrap this antiquity. Sadly for my ego, I had to go to the museum to take photos.

BK— Before Kids

Have you ever had a conversation about the things you used to do before kids joined the family, but don't do now? Our list is endless. Because of the type of parents we have become, not many people would think that we would have done those things before! In this layout I used an old photo of a hot rod we used to own before kids (BK). I listed several activities we used to be involved in, but aren't anymore. The big changes in our lives came about when we had children. But big changes can also occur as a result of accepting a new job, moving, leaving home and starting college, starting a new business venture, overcoming hurdles. The list is endless. Small things can change so quickly because of large changes. Try making pages about some of those **then** and **now** things—the small ones and the big ones.

MONDAY
TUESDAY
Wednesday
THURSDAY
FRIDAY
SATURDAY
SUNDAY

41

I Can't Believe We Used to Do That!

We lost the remote the other day, so we actually had to get up and walk to the TV to change the channel. It **felt** like a huge inconvenience, and in the world of modern technology it was a huge inconvenience. How things have changed. When I was a teenager my TV only had four buttons on the front and didn't have a remote. I used an old stick to reach across the room and press the buttons on the TV. Channel 1, 2, 3 or 4. Can you believe that?

There are plenty of things that have changed over the years that bring great amusement to those who weren't there, or those who simply had forgotten about them. This section concentrates on those memories. When you hear yourself or someone else say, "Can you believe we used to do that?" consider capturing the story on a layout.

Pages inspired by these thoughts will often have a humorous tone. It's fun to laugh at days gone by, to make fun of the way we used to do things. Photos might not be available, but as in the layout "No Remote" we can take pictures of the modern equivalent of the subject of our page. It doesn't really matter, as long as the story is there.

No Remote

Me: (to Paul) Do you remember our first T.V.? It only had 4 buttons on the front for different channels.

Paul: But there were only 3 channels available.

Me: *cracking up* Yea seriously – only 3 channels.

Paul: And no remote.

(Jacob standing listening to conversation with the 'I don't believe you' look on his face)

Paul: And we had this big long stick to try and reach the buttons on the front of the T.V. to change the channel.

Me:: To save getting out of the chair and walking to the T.V. to change it.

Paul: *laughing* Yea, no remote.

Jacob: You two are kidding right? You are making a joke right?

Me: No seriously! We didn't have remotes! We used a stick!!

Jacob: (Unbelieving) you guys are sooo funny.. No remote.. Yea right

no reMote

10 OCT 2006

MONDAY

TUESDAY

Wednesday

THURSDAY

FRIDAY

SATURDAY

SUNDAY

Feb 1996

Whatever happened to *Style?*

one week

as a mother, 30 years apart. It wasn't until I became a mother that I really paid attention to this glamorous photo of my mum with her first child. How on earth did she fit back into that dress? And those shoes? At one week, I was barely out of my pyjamas! Mum says it was just what they did back then, and I'm sure it wasn't very comfy. But it would be so worth it for that picture!

Jan 1965

One Week
Loretta Grayson

Comparing photos of the same Life Event—then and now—can dramatically highlight how things have changed. Loretta's layout is a classic example. The photos of her mother and herself were each taken one week after having a baby. As Loretta explained in her journaling, the way her mother presented herself in a pre-pregnancy dress and looking like she had never had a baby, was just the way things were done back then. As hard as it is to believe now, the photo provides the stylish proof!

MONDAY

TUESDAY

Wednesday

THURSDAY

FRIDAY

SATURDAY

SUNDAY

Pink

Sometimes it's not a physical thing that sparks the thought, "I can't believe we used to…." For us, it was the recent realization of how things have changed since a daughter joined our family. For the longest time, even after she was born, we didn't think we'd see **pink** in our home. I grew up with two brothers and so I was not a girlie-girl. We had two sons first, so our world was full of boy stuff and blue. I distinctly remember telling a friend there was no way I was going to succumb to the stereotypical pink that having a daughter can bring. I was wrong; my world is now filled with pink. I can't believe I ever said it wouldn't be!

Curls
Linda Albrecht

When thinking about "things she couldn't believe she used to do," Linda remembered the curlers she used to wear and wear and wear as a youngster. During our e-mail exchange on the topic, Linda and I compared **curler stories**. Creating the layout "Curls" brought back vivid childhood memories for Linda. My stories were based on seeing my grandmother put curlers in her hair, a cap over the top and plug a huge hose into the cap to blow hot air inside to dry her hair. I agree with Linda—thank goodness for the inventor of the curling iron!

When I Was Little

Fond memories of curling up by the fireplace in the wintertime, of childhood companions and of summertime rituals come to mind if I hear the words, "When I was little…."

Some of the most special times during my husband's childhood took place during summer holidays at the beach. He often refers back to those times in conversation, and it is always with fondness. Christmastime barbeques on the beach late into the evening, meeting new friends at the beach, swimming all day and scouring the shoreline for treasures. These experiences added up to what Paul describes as "some of the best summers ever."

When I talk with him about these times, there isn't usually a lot of detail. He remembers the whole experience, and it is one he wants to give to his own family. I didn't have any photos of Paul at the beach when I created the layout "Beach Tradition." Because Paul had referred to the experience as one he wanted to give to his own children, I used modern photos of our children making memories at the beach.

We all have our own "When I was little…" experiences. Whether they are not-so-fond memories, or whether they are times that are remembered with love, they are all of interest to those who read our scrapbooks. These experiences from our childhood imprint themselves on our personalities and goals for the future and become part of the very essence of the people we are today.

Beach Tradition

Beach tradition

"Some of the most special times when I was growing up were at the beach. Every summer holidays we would pack up after Christmas and go to the beach for 3 weeks. There was nothing but us, the beach and exploring nature. We socialised with other people there. We would swim all day and we would have BBQs on the beach each evening. I looked forward to it for weeks before we went every year, and I relived every summer moment for weeks afterwards.

These are the kind of memories I want to create for our family. Let's make it a family tradition to go to the beach every year in the summer."
(Paul, 2003)

"Sure, sounds good to me," I said.

1 0 JAN 2006

MONDAY

TUESDAY

Wednesday

THURSDAY

FRIDAY

SATURDAY

SUNDAY

Some people find the sound of the wind and rain down the chimney annoying. I find it comforting. I guess it comes from when I was young. My Mum and Dad owned an old home, they had a new wood burner that went through to the hallway and the chimney was right outside my bedroom door. There was nothing cosier in the winter nights of my childhood than being curled up safe in my warm bed with the wind and rain beating down that chimney. On extra wintery nights I would be treated to hail rattling down. And I'd doze back off to sleep, cosy in my bed. I still love that sound. On extra wintery nights, you will find me cuddled by the fire, loving the sound of the wind and rain down the chimney.

Winter Comfort

It doesn't take long during a wild winter night before I gravitate toward the fireplace. I find comfort in the rattle of the rain and the howl of the wind down the chimney. My family knows that on a cold, rainy day they will most likely find me near the fireplace, but I guess they don't know the full story of why. It is something that stems from my childhood and the nights I spent tucked into my warm bed while listening to the weather howling down the chimney. My gravitation toward the fireplace will probably be a lifelong habit for me. My scrapbooks are the perfect place to document just why that spot is so special.

Looking Back

I've heard the stories for years. I have heard my dad talk of arriving via ship to New Zealand and then traveling via ship to return to England for a holiday. It took five weeks to travel each way. That is incomprehensible to me. But while the stories of the big things like voyages on ships need to be recorded, so do the little things. My favorite story of Dad as a child is one he tells about riding his bike. Riding a bike as a child is something most of us can relate to. We like to read about the older generation and feel like we share something in common. I love the story about my dad filling the handlebars on his bike with boiling water to keep his hands warm on the ride to school. The fact that he had to ride miles to school not only gives an insight as to how expectations of children were different back then, it also gives a glimpse into my father's personality.

I returned home to England with my Mum for a holiday. It took us 5 weeks on a ship to get there, and 6 weeks on a ship to return.

It used to be so cold in Pukekohe when I was at high school that I filled the handlebars on my bike up with boiling water and rode 6km to school each day.

When petrol was short in the 1970's we used to have 'Carless days'. Each person designated a day when they would not drive their car. They had a sticker to put on their windscreen showing this day and were fined if they drove on that designated day.

We didn't have TV. There was only 1 channel available and I used to go to the home of a family friend to watch TV, as did every one else. The TV was black and white and they had an optional extra in the way of a screen that hung in front of the TV. The screen was blue on the top and green on the bottom and something else in the middle. The Lone Ranger used to look real funny on his white horse.

John. 1958.

i dug out an old photo of heidi the other day. she was a present for my 8th birthday and a constant companion as i was growing up we were side by side for years. she slept just outside my room and i fell asleep every night to the sound of her snoring. she stayed outside during the day and i would return home from school to her little nose poking out under the gate waiting for me to feed her and take her inside.

i studied a lot throughout my teenage years. in the winter days heidi would lie on my feet, serving the purpose of a forever-warm hot water bottle and constant company. we spent every hour that i was at home in each other's company.

i was 18 years old when heidi passed away. she has been gone 16 years now but i still miss her. i think of her fondly on cold winter days when i am sitting at my desk scrapbooking. i wrap a blanket around my legs and wish i had heidi there to keep my feet warm, but also as the great companion she was for all those years.

heidi

Heidi

Not many people know about Heidi, my closest childhood companion. My childhood pet does not come up in conversation often, although she was a part of my life every day for over ten years. Sometimes I still miss her. Certain times of the year, even sixteen years after she has passed, will remind me of her. So I created a layout dedicated to Heidi, describing the profound effect she had on me as a child. Whether it's a brother, sister, parent, coach, friend, teacher or pet, most of us have someone who affected our lives in a large way. Who would it be for you?

Thursday

As we progress through the week, I find the children are showing signs of being tired. Thursday and Friday often bring more tears around home because of the little things. Stomping feet and arms thrown in the air are par for the course. I am left to mop the tears and sort the fights. These times often lead to long talks with my children.

I love it when the children really get to talking, not just the what-we-did-today kind of stuff, but the real nitty gritty what-I-want-to-be-when-I-grow-up stuff. Keeping a straight face while my son tells me secrets about who he wants to marry and the kind of job he wants to have when he grows up is an art in itself.

And who says he can't do these things? I must have had similar aspirations when I was young. Vaguely, I remember formulating a plan to drive a fire engine with my brother. He told me he would drive the front, and I could drive the back. I agreed and held onto that goal for years—I suspect mainly because of my admiration for my older brother. But whatever the reasons, it is a wonderful story I would love to have had in an album.

Our thoughts about the future cover a range of emotions. From our goals and objectives to our fears and expectations, it all matters a great deal. The pages we create could help affirm the goals we want to achieve, or perhaps they could show us how we overcame possibilities we were dreading in our future. Whatever the circumstances, we should embrace the significance of scrapbooking these thoughts and feelings about everyday moments in the future.

Goals

We all have goals, aspirations and hopes for the future. Sometimes these goals are big, like the decision about which career you want to pursue, a change in the place you live, or whom you live with. Sometimes we turn to people around us for advice on our hopes and dreams. Sometimes we write down these goals. Sometimes, though, these hopes for the future are presented to us in the form of little gems planted in conversation on an otherwise ordinary day.

I have always rocked our eldest son in the lounge in our home when he is feeling down or needs to talk. Although he is nearly eight years old, he always finds room to sit on my knee and cuddle into me. During one of our latest rocking sessions, the thought came to me that he really is getting physically too big for this, and that I'll miss it terribly when he stops this one-on-one attention with me.

What followed was a conversation that started out on a fairly deep and meaningful level, about the feelings of safety that home and being on my knee bring. Jacob declared that he will always want to be with me, even when he is grown up. (Enjoy this while he is young, right?) But what followed was the thing that really spurred me to scrap the moment. Jacob declared, "And since I am grown up, I can drink PowerAde whenever I like. Right, Mum?" What better reflection of Jacob's short-term goals than that sentence. I guess at that moment there wasn't anything much more important than that! Ahhh, the innocence of a seven-year-old!

Write down things your children say they want to do when they are older, especially the amusing things! Or take a quirky look at life from your pet's point of view and make their **predictions** for the future. Write down the things your partner, friends or relatives say about their goals for the future. Wherever the words and thoughts come from, they give us a glimpse into our tomorrow and can lead to meaningful layouts.

PowerAde

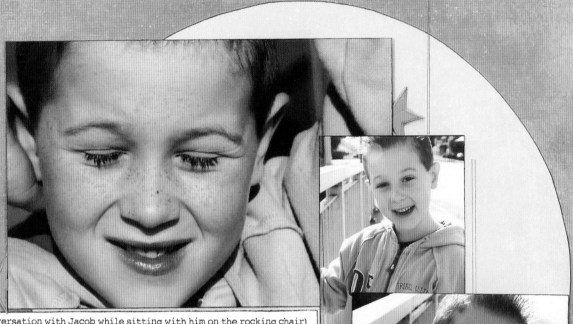

(Conversation with Jacob while sitting with him on the rocking chair)

Me: "Will you still want Rock-Rocks when you are older, Jakey?"

"You know there is nothing better than rock-rocks with Mum."

Jacob: "Yes there is. Home Sweet Home. Home is better – home is where the rock-rocks are."

Me: "When you are older will you have your own kids and rock on the rocking chair with them?"

Jacob: " No. Wait, Yes. If I can live at home with you, that is. "

Jacob: "And since I am grown up I can drink PowerAde whenever I like, right? "

POWERADE

September 2006.

MONDAY

TUESDAY

WEDNESDAY

Thursday

FRIDAY

SATURDAY

SUNDAY

a list of goals

before forty

A 6M+ HARDTOP WEST COASTER BOAT

A SECTION AT THE BEACH

TIME TO SPEND IN THE BOAT.

FOR MY KIDS TO ENJOY MY HOBBIES WITH ME.

YA KNOW? JUST THE FUN STUFF.

(OK SO HAPPY, HEALTHY, THAT COUNTS TOO)

Before Forty

While looking through some papers in a drawer the other day, I found a note my husband had written. I remember when he wrote it. I asked him to write down some goals he hoped to achieve before he turned forty. He scribbled down four or five things, we laughed about the possibility of them ever coming true and the piece of paper was thrown into the drawer. Finding the paper now was like finding a treasure. The sentences Paul wrote on the paper not only gave insight into his life at the time he wrote the note, but also his hopes for the future.

Vet
Caro Huot

Often the goals we hear from our children concern what they want to be when they grow up. With hopes of becoming a vet and treating all sorts of wild and exotic animals, Bea told her mum she also wants to treat insects. No amount of explaining will make Bea understand that entomology is a completely different career. What a fun example of the innocence of youth!

So I've Been Thinking
Linda Albrecht

For her journaling, Linda used a conversation with her son about what he wants to be when he grows up. When he was younger, Cort wanted to be a policeman, but as he grew and his perspective changed, his career choice changed also. The page reflects facets of Cort's personality, including his current interests and where he thinks he is heading with his hobby.

MONDAY
TUESDAY
WEDNESDAY
Thursday
FRIDAY
SATURDAY
SUNDAY

Expectations

We all have plans for the future, but the real fun comes from hearing children give their honest expectations of what our world will be like in days to come. Although our own expectations are worth noting, children just seem to be more creative with how they think the world will be, and what their place will be within it. Take the candid conversation I had with my son the other day....

I started by asking Braden what he planned to be when he grew up. I hoped he would divulge his hidden thoughts about what he thought the world would be like when he was grown. I had preconceived expectations that spaceships and silver suits would come up during our conversation, but Braden surprised me.

He spoke in a more reserved fashion, as he talked of having two sons and a wife with long hair. I was relieved to hear he would invite me to dinner at his house, and he planned to bake mince pies for me. The conversation went on a bit further, but it wasn't long before he went off-subject and started talking with his father. So I quickly wrote down our conversation, before it was forgotten. I love that I got these thoughts written down and that I have this dialogue in my scrapbook. I also love that he (and possibly his future partner!) can look back at it in years to come and laugh. And I'm very pleased to have proof that he said he would invite me over for dinner when he is older!

In a similar fashion, try writing down comments about future expectations that your family and friends share with you. Really listen to their conversations to catch those seemingly ordinary things that they say. We don't always expect the best of the future, and some of our layouts will portray this. That's okay, too. It's all part of our everyday thoughts and emotions.

Five

{ What will the future

be like when you are older?

I'll be a Dad.

There will be houses but no toys.

I will have short hair and long pants.

I will have 2 sons: Jake and Brock.

My wife will have long hair.

We will play rugby together. Outside.

My house will have a big fence around it.

I will have a car; it'll look the same as now.

It will be red. A big red car.

I will make my lunch and take it to work.

Yoghurt, banana and sandwiches.

five 5

I will invite you to dinner and I will make you mince pies.

I think the world will be the same but there will be no leaves.

And no cutty grass either.

November 3 2006

MONDAY
TUESDAY
WEDNESDAY
Thursday
FRIDAY
SATURDAY
SUNDAY

Thomas: "Mum, when I am big and have a job that earns one thousand dollars I'll give it to you so you can buy me a new scooter."

Me: "You would have a lot of money left over then sweetie, with that kind of money you could buy twenty scooters. Is there anything else that you really want?"

Thomas: "Good, you should buy me twenty scooters! Then I'd always have a new one if it breaks down and I wouldn't have to walk anywhere ever again."

I couldn't help but get this image in my head of you all grown up, dressed in a suit, pulling your scooter out of the garage, ready to go to work.

twenty SCOOTERS

Scooters

Marieke Broekman

It's a classic scenario—the child places himself in the future in his thoughts but forgets that he grows up. I love this! Marieke created a page about Thomas, who loves his scooter. Thomas tells his mum that he is going to grow up and earn money, enough for twenty scooters! What Thomas doesn't realize is that priorities change as we grow. This layout captures Thomas' youthful innocence in all its beauty.

MONDAY
TUESDAY
WEDNESDAY
Thursday
FRIDAY
SATURDAY
SUNDAY

Lesson 2

Expectations

Paul and I made the decision years ago not to travel. We chose the buy-our-own-home-get-a-large-mortgage-at-20-years-old-because-we-can-always-travel-later option. It seemed so right at the time. But who counted on the world becoming so crazy? Ten years ago you could get on a plane and smoke cigarettes all the way to your destination and you were given real cutlery. You could take whatever you liked on the plane. The freedom of a pre-9.11 world. How innocent we were. I'm not sure those travel plans we had are still in place. It saddens me, but who knows what the world will be like by the time we save enough money to board that plane. I talked to a friend recently who was travelling back to the U.S.A. after visiting here. The security measures had been increased yet again – only clear plastic bags allowed on board planes, no liquids – the list of restrictions was huge. " Dude", she said " This is SUCH a Crazy world now – SUCH a Crazy World". I couldn't agree more. September 11, 2006.

CRAZY WORLD.

Crazy World

Many of our expectations for the future are built around goals—such as the goals I illustrated on this page about travel. With the world around us changing daily, it is natural that my expectations will also change. My goal of traveling in the future has stayed the same, but my perception of what it will be like when the future finally gets here has changed.

Anticipating the Future

Anticipating the future can be a scary thing. It can be exciting, too. We all have these feelings. We all feel excitement, anxiety, anticipation or reservations about upcoming events. Whether it is a large event such as a child's first day at school, a job interview, or buying a new car, or whether it is an everyday occurrence that makes us excited or nervous, recording these feelings shares our thoughts with others. The events themselves may or may not be experiences we will scrap, but our feelings about these events reflect a lot about our inner selves.

Currently, one of my main apprehensions is my son growing out of being my **baby**. He's a big kid and getting bigger. I won't be able to pick him up to hug him forever. We often don't realize this kind of opportunity is passing until it's gone, and I'm dreading the day I realize I haven't picked him up for a hug in a while. Braden has no idea I feel apprehensive about this, and he had no trouble coming up with a solution. However, it doesn't change the way I feel. Scrapping these feelings acknowledged my fear and allowed me to put down on paper what words alone could never say about the way I feel for my son.

It's not only feelings for our children that are important though. As we go about our daily lives, there are so many experiences and emotions that we anticipate. Whether they are happy or sad, exciting or fearful, get them on paper. It will be a positive thing to look back on in the future.

growing TOO BIG

The doctor weighed you the other day. 27kg. "Far out," I thought, "and I still pick this boy up off the floor and hug him?" I guess that won't last long. I'll be sad to see the day when you are too heavy for me to lift.
I told you this the other day. "It's Ok", you said, "You don't have to lift me, I'll just stand on the couch and hug you".

I'm glad you have a plan for coping with it. October 2006.

(Layout named 'Growing Too Big' by Brady – Oct '06)

MONDAY

TUESDAY

WEDNESDAY

Thursday

FRIDAY

SATURDAY

SUNDAY

Thirty Seven Rolls of toilet paper.

Thirty Seven

WHY do we have thirty seven rolls of toilet paper in the cupboard?

It's kinda funny. People laugh. But the truth is that I'm just

Following orders

New Zealand Government public announcements in March this year advised preparation for

The Bird Flu

This included stocking up on water, canned foods, facemasks, prescription medication, painkillers, contact numbers of those around you, and

Toilet paper

So hopefully the bird flu may never reach pandemic proportions that they are predicting might happen. We may never see it here in New Zealand. But the New Zealand government is preparing

And so I am preparing

Because I have thirty seven rolls of toilet paper in my cupboard

Thirty Seven.

Thirty-Seven

I remember the dramatic lead-up to the year 2000. The government had us filling our baths with water and stocking up on food and essentials. Soon afterward the fuss of Y2K was forgotten. And we laugh about it now, well, at least about the details we can remember. We are once again being instructed by the New Zealand Government to take precautionary measures—this time in regard to the predicted Bird Flu Pandemic. I have made changes in our home. I have stocked up on essentials and followed their instructions. All three of my children think it is hilarious that our bathroom cupboard is overflowing with toilet paper. Years to come, when one of them has a fleeting memory of their **crazy** mother stashing away so many household necessities, this layout will ensure that we all remember the reasons behind the **madness**.

There's No Such Place As Far Away
Jessie Baldwin

Jessie created this page as both a recognition of the apprehension she felt about a close friend moving away, and also as a reassurance that their friendship will not change. Scrapping this page is a therapeutic way for Jessie to deal with her feelings, and to remind them both that their friendship will endure the distance.

Big Wide World
Loretta Grayson

Loretta's layout shows excitement and nervousness as she assesses her goals for the coming years. Her initial goal of traveling the world with babes in tow has changed, as she now prefers the familiarity of home. The layout not only reveals her plan for upcoming years, but also explains why past ambitions have changed.

MONDAY
TUESDAY
WEDNESDAY
Thursday
FRIDAY
SATURDAY
SUNDAY

For me, Friday is the end of the working week.

It is also the last day of school for the children. I send them off with smiles, because as much as they love being with their friends at school, they love being at home, too. I also send them off each Friday on a mission to search their desks and book bags for missing socks. The weekend is a huge laundry time for me, and I can't wash socks if they are still having a little sock party in the kids' desks at school.

Friday is the day when I look forward to the weekend—the time when I have the people I love around me. We usually don't have anything special happening on the weekend. We spend our time completing jobs and just hanging out at home. People come and go, neighbors stop and chat while we are gardening or watching the kids play out in front of the house. The kids play at various houses in the neighborhood. It is a relaxed time made perfect by the people I'm spending my weekend with. Friday is when I anticipate this time.

If we take a look around us, we can see that we come into contact with many people. Whether we are single, have a partner, have children or grandchildren, or spend most of our days at work or the office, the people that surround us affect us in multiple ways. Whatever our circumstances, this chapter is designed to help us notice those people around us who contribute to our average day.

MONDAY

TUESDAY

WEDNESDAY

THURSDAY

Friday

SATURDAY

SUNDAY

Who Is in My Day?

Who is in your day? At first thought, you might think the list is fairly short. But really think about it. Get out your notebook and pen and write down the people in your typical day. Start with family and then list work colleagues, neighbors, friends, tutors, teachers, coaches, etc. The list is endless, right down to that UPS man you hope will knock on your door with a package each day. Write down every one you make contact with during your day. Your world really does extend further than family and friends.

However, nothing is ever constant and these same people won't always be around you. I can remember neighbors, when I was young, that I loved to hang out with. I don't remember many details about them now and we don't have any photos.

This is an illustration of why we need to identify the people around us and dedicate artwork to the role they play in our day-to-day living. We need to make an effort to take our cameras to the places they will be. Don't stop at creating pages simply about the person though. When you think of those people, is there a common interest or a shared fun situation you can reflect on? Is there a shared joke or a story about the way they helped you or influenced your life that could be told?

Our good neighbors, the Cruickshanks, have a cherry tree. We have a little sweepstake between our families each year to guess the date of the first blossoms. I could do a page about the Cruickshanks and the fact they are our neighbors and how much we adore them, but a page about the cherry tree and our sweepstake shows a depth of meaning to the relationship in a much more revealing way.

Spring Blossoms

september 24
spring
blossoms

We've known the Cruickshanks since they bought our home 10 years ago. As it happened we moved back into the street and have become their neighbours. We share a chat, an occasional wine and I love a walk around their garden – it's so much fun to see what has become of the plants Paul & I planted 10 years ago. One of our favourite things in their garden is the Awanui Cherry Trees. Every year we have a little sweepstake to try and guess what date the first flower will bloom. This year John guessed Sept 24th, I guessed Sept 26th and Paul guessed October 1st. No one was near right; the cherry trees surprised us all by announcing spring early, on the 4th September. I made sure I wrote that one in my diary and I look forward to the friendly neighbour sweepstake again next year. *2006*

Good Times

Adrienne Looman

What can be better than a job you enjoy? How about a job that offers, as a bonus, a ton of fun conversation and good times throughout the day? In her layout, Adrienne describes how the people around her make each day fun. She included snippets of conversation from an average day to let us have a taste of her life at work.

Close Distance
Caro Huot

When taking note of those people in your day, remember the ones you have contact with but don't necessarily get to see person-to-person. Caro's sister Nathalie is an integral part of every day for Caro. Instead of focusing her layout on how much her sister means to her, Caro concentrated on how she communicates with her sister. It's a clever way of showing the small details of their relationship.

My sister Nathalie and I live in the same town, 10 minutes away by car. So.... how come I've only been to her place twice in the past year?! Honestly, we ARE close, I swear!!! Although we don't see each other often, we must talk on the phone every single day. Some days, we'll spend 2 hours on the phone together, and other days we can call each other up 5 or 6 times! And (yes I realize this will sound pathetic) we even call each other during our favourite TV shows' commercials, to gab about what just happened! I talk to her while surfing the web (sometimes we'll both go to the same websites at the same time and talk about it), doing chores (or procrastinating), eating, scrapbooking... We talk about everything. I love that we're this close now. We've always loved each other, but with nearly 8 years between us, our relationship wasn't always the same. Although, mind you... she may be the oldest, I've been known to be more mature at times (even she tells me so). I think that has a lot to do with me having a child long before she did. My youngest 2 kids are the same age as hers, so we can totally relate! It's nice to have someone to call up anytime I have something on my mind, or even when I have absolutely nothing to say! Teehee!!! :)

Neighbour

It would have been so easy to create a page about Jonathan, how much fun he is and how much my children enjoy his company. But I decided to use a different approach. Before I took the photos, I asked my children what they really liked about Jonathan. I asked the boys to describe what they play and how much fun they have. The list of names they came up with to describe their friend was hilarious. I used those words to make the kids laugh in the photo shoot that followed, and then included the same words on my layout.

MONDAY
TUESDAY
WEDNESDAY
THURSDAY
Friday
SATURDAY
SUNDAY

You Are Just Like Your...

It's no joke. I love carbohydrates. Really, I could live on the stuff—pasta, fries, chips, potatoes. If I were creating a menu, it would probably read "all things white and bad for you." I see nothing wrong with that. Right? Okay, so maybe it's not so right. The evil Diet Witch would have a field day in my pantry and fridge. However, it wasn't until my daughter starting preferring the same types of foods that I realized we really are a product of our parents and those around us. This seems to include inheriting others' bad eating habits! It was so easy to set up a photo shoot for this page. One toddler, a bag of chips and myself. Bliss.

Seriously, though, it is a good idea to get these similarities onto our scrapbook pages. I'd love to know how much my grandmother was like her grandmother, or how my dad is similar to his dad, or where any of my family got their noticeable quirks. I'd love to know just where my carbohydrate cravings came from, especially now that I know where they are headed.

I notice the little things about my children that are just like Paul or myself. Then I jot them down in my inspiration notebook to encapsulate later in a layout. I ask family members to point out ways that I am the same as my mum or dad and ways my children are just like me. In the future our family will find it both amusing and interesting to read about the seemingly mundane, everyday things we do, and learn we inherited those quirks from people around us.

Carbo Girl

CARBO girl

I have never been one to like many different foods. It takes a lot of persuading to get me to step outside my basic 'potato and pasta comfort zone' to try something new. I love anything plain. I love potato. I love hot chips. I love pasta. I love breads. I love all those nasty carbs. It seems Abby might be following in my footsteps. As I served her dinner the other night, she took one look at her plate and said, "I don't like this!" as she took the unwanted foods off her plate and dumped them on the bench. It was quickly followed by a "Where's the pasta?!" Paul just cracked up. Like mother, like daughter it seems. It looks like Abby will be a carbo girl just like her Mum. Oct 06.

we love carbs!

MONDAY
TUESDAY
WEDNESDAY
THURSDAY
Friday
SATURDAY
SUNDAY

do chromosomes contain joker genes?

is silliness genetic?

does the genome encode quirky qualities?

JOKER genetics

i look at these photos

my grandfather,

my father &

me ...

and i know the answer has to be yes!!

Joker Genetics
Amelia McIvor

Amelia started showing signs of the **joker gene** at a young age. Whether it was pulling faces or doing silly dances, there were always plenty of laughs when the camera came out at family events. Photos through the years clearly prove she inherited this habit from her father and grandfather. Needless to say, the photos on Amelia's heritage pages are a great source of laughter for everyone in the family.

MONDAY
TUESDAY
WEDNESDAY
THURSDAY
Friday
SATURDAY
SUNDAY

Lesson 2

You Are Just Like Your...

Competitive
Kelly Goree

When I suggested to Kelly that she do a page on similarities her oldest son has with his father, it was easy for her to choose an aspect of their relationship to scrapbook. They both love to play games. They both have a competitive nature. And they both love to win!

You Can Always Count On...

Friends are some of the most important people in our lives, yet we often take them for granted. We pick up the phone and call them, or we drop by their house on the assumption that they will always be there. Lucy is a friend I can always count on to be there in good times and bad, for the huge events in my life and for the little things. Despite the large amount of time we spend together, there were very few photos of us together.

Recently we took the time to get together for a photo shoot, which turned out to be hilarious. As per usual for Lucy and me, we had trouble staying serious. One of the funniest photos in the shoot was the one that I wasn't even in! Naturally I knew the reason why I was missing from the shot, but in years to come no one else would know. So of course I chose that picture to scrap. It shows the relationship I have with one of the most important people around me. Friendship pages don't always have to show loving sentiment in obvious ways. Sometimes it is the photo shoot outtakes that show the **real** relationship.

Always True Friends

I love that we can laugh at the little things

I love that we can share the important things.

It's cool that we have a combined love of scrapbooking

We enjoy hanging out together

I would have been in this pic with you.

always...

Except I'm not — because you just pushed me over.

Which just goes to show what good friends we are.

TRUE FRIENDS

MONDAY
TUESDAY
WEDNESDAY
THURSDAY
Friday
SATURDAY
SUNDAY

You don't see dust.
(Dust haunts my every day).

You don't feel guilty for days before going away. (I feel the need to organise and feel guilty for weeks)

A good steak can make your day. (It takes a successful day scrapping to make mine)

You don't feel the cold. (I'd have the fire going all day if I could)

Your have to have meat on your sandwiches. (As long as there is vegemite & chips on there, I'm happy)

You listen to the sports radio stations. (I listen to Alanis, James Blunt & Jack Johnson)

You can't think about dinner til dinnertime. (I think all day about what I have to organise for dinner).

the **man** *mind*

i love you

Hahei March 2006

The Man Mind

The Man Mind is something that has been discussed by women for years. Whether it is a co-worker, a son, a brother, father or husband, the Man Mind and its intricacies are something we can always rely on. I admit I have my share of grievances with the way Paul's mind works. We think about some things so differently. Like the way he cannot see dust. Like the way the radio is always tuned to a sports station after he drives my car. Like the way he doesn't seem to have the Mummy Guilt I endure. These differences are also the everyday things I can count on to make him the person he is. The small annoying things can lead to a humorous layout and deserve to be recorded along with the good things.

Something I Can Always Count On
Adrienne Looman

Adrienne's day is not complete without cleaning up something Bruiser destroyed while she was away at work. From flowers to string, from toilet paper rolls to clothing, Bruiser is guaranteed to add that little bit of "what-will-he-have-destroyed-when-I-get-home" mystery to Adrienne's day. Adrienne has plenty of pages dedicated to how much she adores Bruiser. So it is perfectly fitting to dedicate a page to the everyday stuff. These are the things that make us smile—or not!

Trash 2 Treasure
Marieke Broekman

When Marieke takes her children to visit their grandmother, it is obvious where they get their fascination for interesting bits and pieces. With their Oma looking on, they sit and play with everything from toilet paper rolls, to cotton reels to toothpaste lids. Although it's a small detail in an adult's day, it is something the children will remember as a big deal. Having a grandmother who they could always count on for such interesting fun is something they will want to look back on in times to come.

MONDAY
TUESDAY
WEDNESDAY
THURSDAY
Friday
SATURDAY
SUNDAY

Saturday

MONDAY

TUESDAY

WEDNESDAY

THURSDAY

FRIDAY

Saturday

SUNDAY

Looking outside, the weather is yucky. Roll on summer. Who needs the severe gale-force winds and the inside out umbrellas that graced the soccer park today when I drove past? (**Who**, I mean, **who** opens an umbrella with wind like this? Seriously. Isn't it basic physics? Force of wind greater than backward pressure of shape of umbrella and **woompa**, umbrella turns inside out. Sometimes I wonder.) However, I digress.

I love where we live. I love New Zealand for all its clean, green beauty. Sometimes I question if somewhere else might be a little more tropical, but then when I look at my environment, when I really look at what is around me, I start to notice all the things that make this a perfect place for me to live.

Our environment isn't just the place we live. It extends so much further. It includes the situations we put ourselves in by living in the home we do. It includes the way we shape our environment to accommodate our hobbies and lifestyle. It includes how we bring the outside world into our home.

Whether we love where we are or are looking for a better place to be, our environment affects us every day. If we turn the tables, the effect we have on our environment is just as important. These are the ordinary things where we will find perfect stories for our scrapbooks.

Take a Look Around You

Take a look around you. Stop what you are doing, get up and really take a look around you. What is it about the environment you have created that makes your home a place where you want to live? Pick up your notebook and start making notes. Look around the room and notice the fruit bowl on the table because you like the kids to always have fresh fruit available. Notice the chewy toys out on the lawn because you decided to include a pet in your family. Take note of the barbeque on the deck because you love to socialize with friends over a barbeque dinner on a hot weekend afternoon.

What things do you make certain remain **constant** wherever you move? What are the things you always seem to surround yourself with? These are the things that have proven to be significant in your life just by being there over and over. They may be conventional everyday things, but they are what make us comfortable in our surroundings.

Our family has moved many times in the past ten years. There are items we make sure we always have when we move into a new home. Some of these items are substantial requirements, some are important to just one or two members of the family, and some are seemingly insignificant. However, they are all reflective of our needs at the time, and for that reason, I choose to identify these requirements and scrap about them.

The page "10 Reasons" was created to celebrate one aspect about our environment that our family loves. We love the freedom of living on a quiet street where the traffic is barely existent and the kids can play beside the road with little danger. I'm sure in years to come the kids will enjoy looking at these pages and better understanding the various reasons we moved when we did.

10 Reasons

MONDAY

TUESDAY

WEDNESDAY

THURSDAY

FRIDAY

Saturday

SUNDAY

1. We can use the road to ride our bikes.

2. We can use the end of the road as one big chalkboard

3. There is always someone to play with.

4. The little kids are welcome to play with the big kids

5. We can draw a tennis court on the road and it washes off with the next shower of rain

6. There is always a neighbour ready for a water fight.

7. We have our own little community down here.

8. We have street parties for fireworks and Christmas. On The road!

9. A borrowed cup of sugar is never far away

10. We don't have to drive home after socialising with friends.. they live right here.

it's not what you look at that matters, it's what you see.
Henry David Thoreau

10 REASONS

Why we love Cul De Sac living.

delight in simple things.

No children were left unsupervised on a road in the making of this layout or in any given day we happily play in our cul de sac.

FAITHFUL *friend*

I feel safe each night as you sleep at the foot of my bed

cold nose... warm heart!

my everyday companion— you are always by my side when I need a friend

you entertain the kids, you make us all laugh, and you snuggle with us when we are sick. You are more than a pet. You are family

good dog!

those big brown eyes— so sweet and so cute!

Faithful Friend
Jessie Baldwin

Jessie and her family love having a pet in their home. They consider Rabbas to be a member of the family, and they wouldn't have it any other way. A pet, who is a part of the family and shares your house and environment, is an integral part of your home and deserves a page all its own.

Feijoa Tree

Feijoas. It is a subtropical fruit that most New Zealanders identify with. When I was a young girl, we had a feijoa tree in our backyard. I remember sitting under the tree with my siblings, on crisp autumn days, scooping the sweet flesh from the fruit. As I have grown up and created my own home surroundings, I find myself wanting a feijoa tree in my own backyard. When I look around, I realize there are certain things that are always important to me when I move into a new home—from the items in the garden to the way the house faces in relation to the sun. The things we value in our environment show who we **really** are and where we've come from.

Wildlife
Lisa VanderVeen

When Lisa took a step back from the corporate world to start a family, her priorities changed and lead her to a property abundant with wildlife. When deciding where to live, she considered different aspects of the surroundings. Her "Wildlife" layout highlights one particular member of the nature community. Lisa's priorities for her surroundings may not always be the same. She may move back to the city and the corporate world in the future. But, whatever happens, it is good to capture the current everyday moments to share in years to come.

MONDAY

TUESDAY

WEDNESDAY

THURSDAY

FRIDAY

Saturday

SUNDAY

Hobbies

As Saturday evening draws near, the atmosphere in our family home changes. One of us seems more on edge. There is pacing and obvious nervousness. There is a Warriors game on tonight, and it electrifies the whole atmosphere of the home. I'm a supportive wife. No, really, I am. I join in on the fun. I support everything about Paul and the Warriors, because it has become an integral part of our family life and home.

Hobbies often reveal central things about our personalities. When we become truly passionate about something, it affects who we are, the reasons we do things and the people around us. Our moods are affected by how our hobbies are going, and how much time we can spend on our favorite pastimes. Our home might also be affected when our hobbies start to overflow into family space, or take up time that would otherwise be spent with family or friends.

Currently, my children go to my scrap room when they cannot find me; they figure that is where I will be. Similarly, they think that every rugby league game on TV needs to have "Go Warriors!" screamed at it. They are too young to know the difference, and because they see so much of our respective hobbies in their lives, I can understand their reactions to both.

For these reasons I scrap about our hobbies. I journal about what makes me so passionate about my hobby, and how it is incorporated into everyday life and the environment around me. It is something the children will be able to read and relate to in years to come.

Warriors

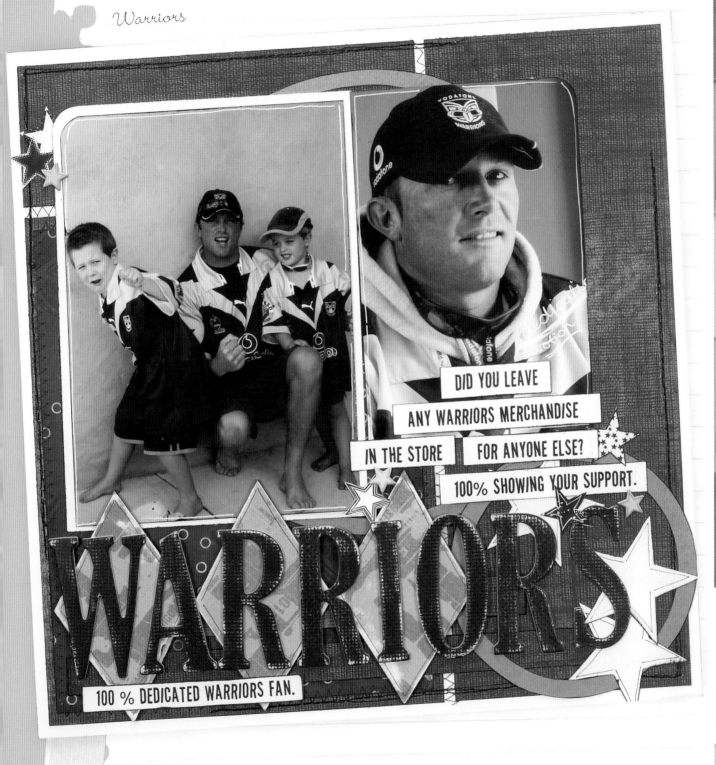

DID YOU LEAVE ANY WARRIORS MERCHANDISE IN THE STORE FOR ANYONE ELSE? 100% SHOWING YOUR SUPPORT.

100 % DEDICATED WARRIORS FAN.

MONDAY

TUESDAY

WEDNESDAY

THURSDAY

FRIDAY

Saturday

SUNDAY

It's the huge joke with Dad... his recent addiction to selling stuff on trademe... If we don't bolt it down we are afraid he might [SELL IT] So far the kids have returned from their grandparents house without being sold...

trademe
ADDICT

Trademe Addict

I admit, on-line sites can be addictive, but I never thought anyone more unlikely to fall into the trap than my father. I fear my kids will think back to visits with their grandparents as experiences of unwrapping courier packages and wading through brown paper packaging to find the new toys that have come in the mail. Not only has Dad found a hobby he loves, but that hobby has taken over his office, his lounge, and his kitchen.

Listen carefully to the sound of play in the Howard home. If there is more than a spare second in the day you can hear the Pokemon battle cry ringing out across the rooms of the Howard home. The Pokemon thing started so suddenly and caught on so quickly. It began with a slight interest in a TV program. It soon moved to a full obsession. From sun up to sundown, Pokemon has become the life purpose of Jacob and Braden. Their whole environment has been taken over by the Pokemon bug. I walked down the hallway at bedtime last night and heard the familiar sound of Pokemon battle, 2 hours after they should have been asleep. I don't know how long this will last but for now, we live and breathe Pokemon. Come out Blastoise. Come out Hitmonchan. Blastoise use Skull Bash! Hitmonchan use Fire punch! Hitmonchan has a quarter left. Blastoise has a half left. Blastoise use hydro pump! Blastoise has defeated hitmonchan! Come out hitmonlee. Hitmonlee use double MEGA KICK! Blastoise use tackle! Hotmonlee has half left. Blastoise is out. Come out Charizard. Charizard use Slash. Hitmonlee is out. Come out Pikachu! Battling with Charizard!

gotta CATCH 'em all. pokemon!

Jacob - August 2006 - Pokemon Fever.

Pokemon

Our home is absolutely overrun by Pokemon right now. There are figurines in my washing machine. There are Pokemon cards scattered around the floor. I greet the boys with a "How was your day?" as they come in the door from school and what comes back at me is a barrage of Pokemon facts. It is as if they couldn't speak their quota of Pokemon while they were at school, so it all overflows as soon as they return home. The Pokemon phase came on fairly quickly, and I'm sure it'll pass just as fast. But for now it is something incredibly significant in our home, so it deserves a place in my scrapbook.

Blue Tab Explosion

Scrapping to me is a personal hobby that is precious. It is at the base of my very soul and has become a large part of who I have become. Unfortunately it has also started to take over my home. Boxes of **stuff** in the hallway. Finished and unfinished projects scattered around on the shelves. Slowly it is creeping around my house in an unpredictable fashion. The milestone moment in my scrapbooking-hobby-creeping-into-the-home records came last week. It took just one sentence for me to realize that my hobby really has taken over. "Mum," said my five-year-old son, "I had one of those blue tabby things in my lunchbox at school today."

blue tab EXPLOSION

a scrapper lives here

MONDAY

TUESDAY

WEDNESDAY

THURSDAY

FRIDAY

Saturday

SUNDAY

The Greater World Around Us

When we think of our environment, we think of our home. As we stand and look around, we see all those things that surround us and accumulate in our living space. We see the obvious physical things, the people and pets, the furniture and possessions and the outside habitat. But there is another interesting aspect that presents itself as our **greater world**—how we extend ourselves outside our home.

Back in 1998, when I first purchased a computer, I had no idea what a huge effect it would have on my personal group of friends and family. Until then things seemed simple. There were work friends, non-work friends and family that I socialized with. All of a sudden the computer opened up the whole world for me.

I now have a network of friends I could never have imagined. My living space has opened considerably as I have invited these people into my day-to-day space through the Internet. There are the people I chat with and e-mail and then there are those who read my blog. That's a whole other story.

Girlfriends

The internet. If you had told me eight years ago that I would meet so many caring, intelligent, inspiring people from all over the globe via computer technology, I really wouldn't have believed you. Here I am, eight years on, and living a blissful online life with the support of ladies from all over the world. From Switzerland, to Canada, Australia and the U.S.A, these are just a sprinkling of the people I love that I have met online. These friends are important as any people I met through school or work or other situations. And so I become dependant on my computer and the internet. It's not just a home appliance any more. It's a window to my outside world.

girlfriends

MONDAY

TUESDAY

WEDNESDAY

THURSDAY

FRIDAY

Saturday

SUNDAY

best FRIEND

Sophie & Elsie were destined to be friends... they were born just months apart. They live just around the corner from each other... their daddies work together... both pastors at the same church... their mommies are the best of friends, dragging them along to the gym everyday... their little brothers are the same age... destined to terrorize them for years. It was fate these girls would be best of friends.

Best Friend
Courtney Walsh

Courtney created a page based on a friendship her daughter made due to the way her family extended itself outside the home. It is easy to notice our family members when we think about the people around us whom we treasure. But Courtney looked further and created a scrapbook page about a friendship between her daughter and a friend's daughter that originated in her church's social circle.

The Greater World Around Us

MONDAY

TUESDAY

WEDNESDAY

THURSDAY

FRIDAY

Saturday

SUNDAY

This is my blog. The Life of a Scrap at Home Mum. The name is perfect; it incorporates the things that take up most of my time right now, scrapping and motherhood. These things don't always leave me much time to do much else and I have found my blog is a perfect way of keeping in touch, yet I don't spend much time online communicating. It is all right there in one place for people to log onto if they like. It's a worldwide thing... I have a brother in Canada. I have one good friend in Hawaii and others scattered all over the world. I have an Auntie in Wellington and another in Australia. I am extending my world through my computer. Welcome to my world. Welcome to the life of a Scrap at Home Mum.

Scrap at Home Mum

At first a blog seemed like an attractive idea because I love to write and it was a place to share my thoughts. I have family all over the world who check in, so what easier way to keep in touch than an open diary on the Internet?! Since starting my blog, however, my world has opened up a **little**. I have people who read my blog daily who I would never have met otherwise. I often talk with my family about the things I learn from people that visit my blog, and "blog" has become an everyday word for my kids. I opened the doors and extended my home environment out to the **greater world** around us.

Life's Little Lessons
and Words of Wisdom

Ideally, Sunday is a day of rest around our home. Perhaps the day will include a little outing. If the weather is fine, it might be a time to hang out with the kids or friends. But if it is raining, we like nothing better than to relax and enjoy what my family calls "DVD and Duvet Day." We love to grab the duvet from the top of the bed and curl up in the warmth watching a favorite movie together.

It's also a day of reflection. It is a day of looking back on the week that has passed. Sunday is a good time to talk with the kids about any major issues they have had at school. And it's a time for Paul and me to talk through any work situations we've dealt with during the week. The talks aren't heavy and serious, but merely a winding down of the week that has been. It is also a time to reflect on the upcoming week. We prepare for the days ahead and talk about situations we may encounter. This is just everyday conversation that might come about on a Sunday, simply because we are more relaxed and get to spend more time with each other.

Life is made up of many ordinary, everyday things. I spend as much time scrapping these things as I can, merely because they are here one day and gone the next. These **little things** mold our personalities and those of the people around us, and they will most certainly be missed when they are gone. And in the bigger picture, these little things can sometimes teach us fairly huge lessons. Hidden in everyday conversation and in the actions of others are sentiments and words of advice that deserve to be remembered. This section is dedicated to life's little lessons and words of wisdom that we can pick up in an ordinary day.

MONDAY

TUESDAY

WEDNESDAY

THURSDAY

FRIDAY

SATURDAY

Sunday

Those Little Things People Say

Those little things people say, sometimes seriously, sometimes in jest, are the snippets of conversation we often hold on to and keep close. Nothing settles in our minds, whether intentional or not, more than little pieces of advice from someone we admire or love.

My decision to do anything significant is often preceded by a chat with my parents. Perhaps not intentionally, but talking about the important stuff just seems to happen naturally when I visit Mum and Dad. There is one day I remember in particular. My book proposal, which was in itself a lot of work, had been accepted by the publisher. I was now a long way into creating the artwork, but had hit a brick wall in the motivation department. I sat and chatted with Mum and Dad about how hard the process was and how I hadn't realized it would be so taxing, not just on me, but on the whole family.

Dad is a straightforward kind of guy. He has some gems of wisdom though. Dad just looked at me and said, "You didn't think it would be easy, did you?" These were wise words. They were words of encouragement. I have to admit that I just sat and looked at him. I had no answer. Point taken. Lesson learned.

You will find there are many words of wisdom hidden in your day as well. Find a little time each day to really listen to those around you. Write down the little things they say that inspire you. You never know when their words might be perfect inspiration for your art and your life.

Easy

"Because your father knows best". How many times did I hear my father say that in the answer to my "why" questions when I was younger? I distinctly remember thinking "Yea yea whatever". 20 years later things have changed a little. I have a family of my own and find myself saying things like "Because your Mother knows best". I have come to accept that perhaps my Dad did know best.

These days I go to my Mum and Dad's place regularly for a chat. Perhaps even to run ideas past them. This particular day I sat and talked about the work for this book and how hard it was and how although I was enjoying it, I really was finding it stressful.

Dad turned to me and said "You didn't think it was going to be

EASY, did you?

6 SEPT 06.

Yes Dad. I guess you are right. This wasn't going to be easy. I'll just get on with it.

MONDAY

TUESDAY

WEDNESDAY

THURSDAY

FRIDAY

SATURDAY

Sunday

Yesterday Braden told me I was beautiful. It melted my heart, as you would expect. I told him to always remember, even when he is a grown up man, that he will always melt a woman's heart

By telling her she is beautiful.

Today Braden came home from school, he was so proud of himself. We had a new teacher today Mum

And I told her she was beautiful.

What did she say, Braden? (I was kind of afraid of the answer) Um just thanks.

Ahhh. Sweet innocence.

bea·u·ti·ful

Beautiful

Like every mother, it's not uncommon for me to slip words of advice my son's way. They are the little things I hope he will remember when he is older. Braden is well known for occasionally returning conversation with gems of wisdom of his own. The innocence of a five-year-old and his conversation with the teacher is not something we will remember forever. We remember our children being cute and we have the photos to prove it, but will we remember those cute little things they say? They are soon erased with the passage of time. These snippets of wisdom from the world of a five-year-old are classic examples of the things we really need to record. Sometimes we learn life's little lessons from the mouths of babes.

Enjoy Her While She Is Young

Ahhh, the wise words from one mother to the next. Where would we be without their valuable input as we raise our children? I have heard many pearls of wisdom. Some I take note of, some I ponder over for a few days, and some barely enter my memory. A few wise words stay in my mind, because I know I'll need to refer back to them in the future. "Enjoy her while she is young." There is a treasured piece of advice. Scrapping these words of wisdom on a layout will show Abby in the future what she was like when she was young, and will offer encouragement to her if she has children of her own.

I am in the lounge. Abby comes running through, pinched between her thumb and forefinger is a piece of cotton. " MUM! Look what I find!" Pieces of cotton are easily found in my home. They are all over the floor. But as I go to take this one out of Abbys hand I see it is a really long one. Imagine my eyes trailing past her and my thought pattern as I see the cotton goes all the way out of the lounge, through the dining room, in fact it just carries on all the way to the sewing machine. What are those words of wisdom? Enjoy the kids while they are young? Enjoy them because they grow all too fast? Sometimes I need reminding.

After watching "Harry Potter and the Sorcerer's Stone", the following conversation took place:

You: "Hey, I know something I want for Christmas!"

Mama: "Oh yeah? What's that, E?"

You: "An Invisibility Cloak!"

Mama: (chuckling)

Daddy: "Well, I don't think an invisibility cloak really exists, but if it did, I think I'd want one, too!"

You: "Why would YOU want one?"

Mama: "Probably for the same reason YOU would, Ethan."

You: (after thinking for a half-second) "Oh, to get Turner??!"

Um, yeah, buddy.....so we can "get" your brother, too!

September 13, 2006

Can You See Me Now?
Kelly Goree

Sometimes we are inspired by the things people say, even when they didn't intend to inspire us. The conversations may be everyday, average stuff that for most people would go in one ear and out the other, but for us it takes on meaning that heartens us. One day, Kelly and her husband were talking with their son, Ethan, and he asked if they would like an invisibility cloak and why. His conversation continued on in the typical way of a young boy as he assumed that his dad would want an invisibility cloak for the same reason he would want one—to get Turner, his brother. Ethan's innocent words are so refreshing. The view from a child's world can be an inspiration to take a step back and look at the world with no strings attached.

MONDAY
TUESDAY
WEDNESDAY
THURSDAY
FRIDAY
SATURDAY
Sunday

97

Things We See That Inspire Us

Inspiration is all around us. I am inspired when I drive down the road and see someone pacing the sidewalk with their iPod on. I could do that, I think; I'd love to be healthier. I am inspired when I go to the grocery store and see well-behaved children using their manners. I want to make an effort to help my children behave like that, I think; I'm sure I could be a better mother. I am inspired when I see someone helping someone else in a random-act-of-kindness way. I want to be more like that, I think; there is a need for more unsolicited charity in the world.

Sometimes the inspiration comes not from outside the home, but from those living with us. Recently we took all three kids on a little outing to a local Pet Day event. They bickered all the way there and by the time they made their way around what seemed to be only three horses, five calves and various noisy chickens, I knew we were set for an equally fun car trip home.

On the way back to the car we passed a playground. I just wanted to get the kids in the car and go home. Paul insisted we let the kids play. So we did. The kids ran to the swings. I admit I was a little jealous, as this playground was the very one I spent hours playing on as a child. Those swings were the same swings I spent my school days on. I stood back with the camera and wished I were a kid again.

At that point, Paul walked straight up to the swings and got on one of them. I didn't seriously think he would swing, but he did. He swung as high as he could and then he let go and jumped off. I want to be more like that, I thought, and worry less about what people around me think. Just another lesson in an ordinary day.

To Be Free

It's a fine day so we take the kids out to the local calf Club day. It's been a typical spring so we are all sick of the wind and rain, we are glad to get out of the house. The Calf Club didn't thrill the kids much but the playground outside the school was a hit. The little swings were a favourite of Braden and Abby, and Jacob took off on a big boy's swing. As per usual, I stood with the camera. This used to be my school and I can remember swinging for hours on those swings. It was cool to see the kids loving them as much as me. I did feel a little jealous, I admit. Sometimes, just sometimes, I'd love to be a kid again. Of course as I'm thinking these things I see Paul jump on to one of the bigger swings, swing really high then come flying off. Everyone was watching. Paul didn't care.
Way to have fun with the kids!
It's not everyone that will jump on a swing and not worry about the world around them watching. Maybe I should take a leaf out of your book, Paul.

inspiration

fun

TO be FreE

OCT 2006

MONDAY

TUESDAY

WEDNESDAY

THURSDAY

FRIDAY

SATURDAY

Sunday

Meet Shauna and her family. Shauna lives is a close friend. Close enough that when she was recently diagnosed with grade 4 cancer – fine one day, grade 4 cancer diagnosis the next - I was devastated. We've been friends for years. A few years back Shauna opened her home to me, I stayed with her family and enjoyed her daily life and routines. I love this girl to bits I can relate to her life, as it is very similar to mine except she is in America, I am in New Zealand. Throughout the weeks following the diagnosis I have watched Shauna go through so much. But then I have watched Shauna pick herself up, dust herself off, and start all over again. She knows that her life will never be the same. She knows she needs to put plans in action in case something happens to her, but she doesnt let it get in the way of what is most important to her. So here we are. October 8th, 2006. Shauna is undergoing regular chemo. She has had to give up her job within the scrapbooking industry and her Mum has had to move in with her to help take care of the family. I cant help thinking over and over how tough it must be. But Shauna is so brave and so courageous. *And so I am inspired* I am inspired to make the most of my time, to live each day. We never know what the next will hold. I seek opportunities and run with them. Because that is what Shauna is doing. And because of this, I admire her.

simple PLEASURES

love you more every day
xoxoxo

Courage

Courage

Sometimes life brings difficulty so hard to deal with that it is almost unbearable, as is the situation with my friend Shauna. The weeks and months after Shauna's diagnosis have been a tough ride for Shauna and her family and friends. And I have been there however I could to support her. I admit, her situation got me down. But then I stood back and looked at how Shauna was handling things and the courage she was exuding. Her attitude and pride are a huge encouragement to me in all aspects of my life.

MONDAY
TUESDAY
WEDNESDAY
THURSDAY
FRIDAY
SATURDAY
Sunday

Lesson 2

Things We See That Inspire Us

trade-off:

One in five people will be affected by mental illness at some stage in their life. Living with someone who suffers from bipolar disorder has had a serious impact on mine. Many times I came close to going it alone, not coping with the stress it brings when you get sick. But I am still here by your side, fighting for our family when illness takes over once again. If it weren't for the therapy we started I don't think I would be. But you've shown a side I hadn't seen before. You are willing to change your life around for the sake of US. Fighting for the life you really want and a better you. And while you learn, adjust and fight your own demons I am changing with you. I am beginning to see the patterns that have shaped my life and am coming to terms with the decisions I made clouded by past experience. Because of your illness I myself am embarking on a whole new, exciting and sometimes terrifying path in life, I am

finding ME

Finding Me
Marieke Broekman

It's a fact of life that we all will encounter difficult times along the path we travel. We can let these things hold us back, or we can embrace them and let them help us grow. Marieke has watched her husband in his personal battles for years. Although times are hard, Marieke has chosen to find inspiration in what she sees in John. The situation will continue to be a struggle for Marieke, but she has managed to get her feelings on paper, which will be an inspiration for herself in times to come.

Learning to Look After Ourselves

There is a saying in our home that I've heard my husband repeat to our sons many times when they were arguing with me in some respect. "If Momma ain't happy, ain't nobody happy. Remember that, son, and you will lead a happy life." I chuckle to myself at my husband's efforts to keep our home happy. And I chuckle even more about the fact that the boys will grow up with that little piece of advice firmly embedded in their personalities. Their future wives can thank their father-in-law some day.

However, it is true. I'm the center of the home. I am the heart of their day. And when I am not happy, the home is not happy. For this reason, I make sure I look after myself.

It all starts with the basics, and for me one of the most basic needs in my day is caffeine. The trouble comes when I don't have caffeine. I'm not sure if it is a good or bad thing that my family knows the signs when I really need to get my daily dose. There is a saying around our home, if I start to get grumpy, "Must be caffeine o'clock!" When the children grow up and move away from home, whether they have partners or flatmates or live in a dorm or alone, they will always remember the heart of the home needs to be happy. If they know to look after themselves, and those around them, then I will have taught them well. The process of this teaching is through the example of how I look after myself. And so, I think it is important to create scrapbook pages about the things that make me happy.

Caffeine O'clock

MONDAY

TUESDAY

WEDNESDAY

THURSDAY

FRIDAY

SATURDAY

Sunday

caffeine o'clock

I don't drink coffee. I drink diet Pepsi at mid-morning.

What happens if I don't get my dose? My head hurts. I get tired.

I start stumbling over my words when I talk.

I lose patience The kids get naughtier. (I think?)

My house gets dirtier. (how *does* that happen?)

I grow 'spikes' (so my husband says) It's a nasty situation.

The whole family knows if it gets to caffeine o'clock and I haven't had my daily dose of diet Pepsi.

I love my family more than anything.

Yet I take myself away from them and bury myself in this book.

But as my hubby (who is a very clever man) once said to me

If mama aint happy, aint nobody happy

And that is so true.

I need to extend myself.   Set myself goals.

Work hard to achieve them.

So when I am happy, the whole home seems to be.

Set a CHALLENGE and achieve it

Two goals achieved at once. (Thanks guys, love you!)

September '06

Set a Challenge

I am of the belief that I work better with a goal or a challenge set before me. I seem to thrive on stress and deadlines; I don't like having nothing specific to do. The people I spend my days with know this is just the way I am, like it or not! Without my family here to support my goals, I would not be able to reach those goals. But without my goals to keep me focused, I could not be there for my family to the best of my abilities. Life's little lessons are everywhere, including in our goals and our dreams. Taking better care of ourselves allows us to take better care of our families.

I Admit

A self-confessed chocoholic, I have no qualms about my habits. I openly confess my dietary sins, except to my family. I believe it's a secret best kept from them. After all, if I confessed to my family the extent of my obsession with the sweeter foods in life, I'd then have to share said foods. I just don't see the point. Looking after myself means indulging in a few treats now and then. People reading my scrapbooks in the future may not know this simply by looking at my photo. By creating a page focusing on some of the things I do to keep myself happy, future generations will get to know the real me.

OK SO I ADMIT IT. I BUY CHOCOLATE WHEN THE KIDS ARE AT SCHOOL AND HIDE IT BEHIND THE FLOUR CONTAINER IN THE PANTRY. IF I RECEIVE CHOCOLATE AS A GIFT, IT GOES IN A SPECIAL HIDING PLACE IN MY SCRAP ROOM. I MAKE MYSELF A MILO AT NIGHT AND TELL PAUL I AM WORKING IN MY SCRAP ROOM. I INDULGE IN MY BIGGEST DOWNFALL. CHOCOLATE DIPPED IN HOT MILO. I HIDE THE WRAPPERS UNDER PIECES OF SCRAP PAPER IN MY RUBBISH. OK, I ADMIT IT. I HIDE MY CHOCOLATE.

I have never been arty. I would sit in art class at school in awe of the masterpieces being created by everyone but me. My project never seemed to be up the standards of everyone else's. I dropped art after 4th form. However during my school years I was always good at creating projects. You know – those assignments where you made a project, a mini book or a scrapbook about a country for geography, or a disaster for history, for example. I would sit for hours drawing creative borders around my pages and lettering across the top. My title pages were always amazing and the placement of any photos or pictures I included showed an early eye for design.

After my school years I studied business. Among the dreary days full lectures about commercial law, economics and accounting my bright spot was the marketing classes. We created and promoted our own products in these classes. This included advertising, and a class project in the form of a book outlining our reasons for using certain colours, shapes and designs in our marketing material. I was in tertiary education heaven. I came in at top of my class and I believe this how my fascination with colour and design truly began.

So we fast-forward 15 years. I am a stay at home Mum with 3 young children. It seems my keen interest in the things I learnt in those marketing classes have hung around. It wasn't until recently that I stopped and really analysed what I am doing. Scrapbooking. I love everything about it! It's a part of every day now. I'm not the only one that finds the fact that I scrapbook ironic. My hubby recently stood and studied one of my pages as I was working the other night. "Back when you were studying accounting and economics I bet you never thought you'd see the day where you'd spend your day so obsessed with paper and glue".
No. No. I can't say I did.

Obsessed

Alongside my personal luxuries and goals, my hobby is equally important. We all need to have something that is our **getaway**. We all need to have an interest we can call our own and **lose ourselves** in. For me it is scrapbooking. As the journaling says, I never for one minute thought I could be so obsessed with glue and colored paper, but I am glad I am. Scrapbooking is my personal retreat. It is something I can truly call my own.

Supply List

The Last Banana 11
Photo by: Andrea Senn, Auckland, New Zealand
Cardstock; patterned paper (BasicGrey, Crafter's Workshop); chipboard letters (Everlasting Keepsakes, Heidi Swapp); chipboard accents (Deluxe Designs); stamps (Fontwerks); rickrack (Li'l Davis); brads (Queen & Co.); solvent ink; acrylic paint; pen; Old Peas font (Two Peas in a Bucket)

I So Can't Take You Seriously (Right Now) 12
Cardstock; patterned paper (We R Memory Keepers); chipboard letters (Everlasting Keepsakes, Heidi Swapp); stamps (PSX); brads (Queen & Co.); acrylic paint; corner rounder; dye ink; pen; Trebuchet MS font (Microsoft)

Monday Morning Alarm 13
Cardstock; patterned paper (We R Memory Keepers); chipboard letters (Making Memories); circle stamps (Little Black Dress); letter stamps (Fontwerks); buttons (unknown); ribbon (Strano); solvent ink; thread; pen; 1942 Report font (Internet download)

Not My Daughter 13
Photos by: June Brown, Pukekohe, New Zealand
Patterned paper (Imagination Project); foam stamps (Li'l Davis); letter and patterned brads (Queen & Co.); acrylic paint; buttons (unknown); dimensional paint; dye ink; Maiandra GD font (Internet download)

Daddy's Home! 15
Cardstock; patterned paper (Scenic Route); chipboard letters (Li'l Davis, Scenic Route); letter stamps (PSX); decorative tape (Heidi Swapp); mesh (Magic Mesh); rub-on accents (BasicGrey); sandpaper; solvent ink; thread; pen; Trebuchet MS font (Microsoft)

You Used to Love Thomas 16
Cardstock; patterned paper (BasicGrey); chipboard letters (Pressed Petals); rub-on letters (Making Memories); star accents (Heidi Swapp); dye ink; pen; My Own Topher font (Internet download); Tasklist font (Two Peas in a Bucket)

Note to Self 16
Cardstock; patterned paper (BasicGrey); brads; chipboard letters (Heidi Swapp); chipboard shapes (Bazzill); letter stamps (PSX); flowers (Queen & Co.); ribbon (KI Memories, Making Memories); acrylic paint; dye and solvent ink; Tahoma font (Microsoft)

Catching Rainbows 17
Patterned paper (BasicGrey, My Mind's Eye); rub-on letters and stitches (Autumn Leaves, Heidi Swapp); brads (Making Memories); tags (OfficeMax); acrylic paint; silver stars (unknown); thread; transparency

Things That Make Me Go Grrr 19
Cardstock; letter stickers (American Crafts, SEI); brads; dye ink; Hot Chocolate font (Two Peas in a Bucket)

Diva Days 20
Cardstock; patterned paper (Fancy Pants); chipboard letters (Pressed Petals); rub-on numbers (Autumn Leaves); solvent ink; Old Type font (Two Peas in a Bucket); Pea Cammi-pea font (Kevin and Amanda)

Trivial 21
Cardstock; fibers, patterned paper (FiberScraps); title letters (Heidi Swapp); rub-on letters (Heidi Swapp, Imagination Project); mesh, tabs (Making Memories); chipboard flowers (Collections Elements); ribbon (Maya Road); stamps (PSX); vellum; solvent ink; pen; Arial Round Bold, Calisto MT fonts (Microsoft)

Who, Me? 21
Cardstock; patterned paper (Chatterbox, Scenic Route); brads; chipboard accent (Fancy Pants); photo turns (7gypsies); pigment ink; corner rounder; Clarence title font (Internet download)

Scrunch Test 25
Patterned paper (Autumn Leaves); acrylic letters, flowers (Heidi Swapp); letter stickers (American Crafts); mesh (Magic Mesh); lace trim (Making Memories); buttons; thread; MS Reference Serif font (Microsoft)

Flared Nostrils of DOOM 26
Photo by: Braden Howard, Pukekohe, New Zealand
Cardstock; chipboard letters, patterned paper, rub-on letters (Scenic Route); letter stickers (SEI); letter stamps (PSX); buttons (Bazzill); beads, flowers (Queen & Co.); chipboard accent (Everlasting Keepsakes); pen; solvent ink; thread

The Great Shoe Debate 27
Cardstock; patterned paper (FiberScraps); chipboard letters (Me & My Big Ideas); brads (Queen & Co.); ribbon (Offray); rub-on accents (Dee's Designs); Avant Garde, Elise fonts (Internet download)

The Order of the Stuff on the Sandwich 27
Cardstock; patterned paper (BasicGrey, Fancy Pants, Imagination Project, We R Memory Keepers); letter stamps (Li'l Davis); letter stickers (American Crafts); rub-on letters (Making Memories); acrylic paint; corner rounder; dimensional paint; eyelets; solvent ink; thread; Fetching font (Two Peas in a Bucket)

Prayer 29
Cardstock; patterned paper (Scenic Route); chipboard letters (Making Memories); chipboard accent (Everlasting Keepsakes); stamps (Autumn Leaves); acrylic paint; corner rounder; flower (Heidi Swapp); pen; solvent ink; Basic, Rickety fonts (Two Peas in a Bucket)

The Plan 30
Cardstock; patterned paper (American Traditional); textured cardstock (FiberMark); chipboard letters (Pressed Petals); rub-on letters (Making Memories); ribbon (unknown); charm (Maya Road); corner rounder; Century Gothic font (Microsoft)

Distracted by the Train 30
Cardstock; patterned paper (BasicGrey, FiberScraps, Scenic Route); chipboard letters (Making Memories); beads, brads (Queen & Co.); glass finish (Plaid); dye ink; Franklin Gothic Book font (Internet download)

Hang Out the Washing 31
Patterned paper (Cosmo Cricket); chipboard letters (Heidi Swapp); stamps (Autumn Leaves); tags (Li'l Davis); pigment ink; pen; Old Type font (Two Peas in a Bucket)

Dishwasher 101 33
Cardstock; patterned paper (CherryArte); chipboard letters (Heidi Swapp); letter stickers (American Crafts); rub-on letters (American Crafts, Making Memories); corner rounder; solvent ink; pen; Tasklist font (Two Peas in a Bucket)

My Car Grows Moss 34
Cardstock; patterned paper (CherryArte, Imagination Project); letter stickers (American Crafts); wooden letters (Li'l Davis); corner rounder; solvent ink; pen; Red Dog font (Two Peas in a Bucket)

Avocado 35
Cardstock; patterned paper, stickers (KI Memories); chipboard letters (Heidi Swapp); patterned transparency (Li'l Davis); solvent ink; pen; Fragile font (Two Peas in a Bucket)

Small Elephant 35
Cardstock; patterned paper (Lazar); mesh (Magic Mesh); chipboard letters (Everlasting Keepsakes, Heidi Swapp, Scenic Route); ribbon (unknown); rickrack (Maya Road); acrylic paint; corner rounder; pen; Screenwriter's Nightmare font (Internet download)

We Were So Cool 39
Photo by: June Brown, Pukekohe, New Zealand
Cardstock; patterned paper (BasicGrey, Imagination Project); chipboard letters (Everlasting Keepsakes); chipboard stars (Deluxe Designs); buttons (unknown); ribbon (Heidi Swapp, Making Memories); tags (BasicGrey); corner rounder; solvent ink; pen; Basic, Hot Chocolate font (Two Peas in a Bucket)

Home 40
Photo by: Lucy Van der Loos, Pukekohe, New Zealand
Cardstock; patterned paper (Greener Pastures, Imagination Project); brads, flowers (Queen & Co.); acrylic paint; dimensional paint; solvent ink; Century Gothic font (Microsoft); Lainie Day font (Internet download); journaling (edited from anonymous e-mail chain letter)

Wow, Really? 41
Patterned paper (Scenic Route); chipboard accents and letters (Everlasting Keepsakes, Heidi Swapp); rickrack, rub-on letters (unknown); acrylic paint; brads (Queen & Co.); corner rounder; solvent ink; thread; Pea Lyndel font (Two Peas in a Bucket)

BK—Before Kids 41
Cardstock; patterned paper (Fancy Pants, We R Memory Keepers); chipboard letters (Pressed Petals); letter stamps (PSX); solvent ink; corner rounder; pen; My Own Topher font (Internet download)

No Remote 43
Cardstock; patterned paper (Crafter's Workshop, Scenic Route); chipboard letters (Heidi Swapp, Scenic Route); stamps (Autumn Leaves); acrylic paint; ribbon (Heidi Grace, May Arts, Queen & Co.); brads, photo turns (Queen & Co.); solvent ink; pen

One Week 44
Cardstock; chipboard letters, patterned paper, sticker (Scenic Route); flowers (Prima); photo corner (Heidi Swapp); buttons (unknown); pen; thread; Century Gothic, Trebuchet fonts (Microsoft); Pegsanna font (Internet download)

Pink 45
Patterned paper (Fancy Pants); chipboard letters, flower (Li'l Davis); stamp (Autumn Leaves); pigment and solvent ink; beads; thread; pen; Secret Garden font (Two Peas in a Bucket)

Curls 45
Patterned paper (Crate Paper, Daisy D's, My Mind's Eye, Scenic Route); chipboard letters (Pressed Petals); acrylic paint; chalk ink; buttons, rickrack, tags (unknown); staples; transparency

Beach Tradition 47
Cardstock; patterned paper (BasicGrey, My Mind's Eye); chipboard letters (Heidi Swapp); corner rounder; glass finish (Plaid); sequins; solvent ink; thread; CAC Shishoni Brush font (Internet download); Red Dog font (Two Peas in a Bucket)

Winter Comfort 48
Cardstock; patterned paper (BasicGrey, Scenic Route); chipboard letters (Li'l Davis); corner rounder; dimensional paint; button, fabric (unknown); pen; Carpenter font (Internet download)

Looking Back 49
Patterned paper (BasicGrey, Hot Off the Press); chipboard accents (unknown); rub-on accents and letters (BasicGrey, Creative Imaginations); watermark ink; pen; My Own Topher font (Internet download)

Heidi 49
Cardstock; patterned paper (Crate Paper, We R Memory Keepers); chipboard letters (Scenic Route); transparent letters (Heidi Swapp); chipboard accents (Everlasting Keepsakes); laser-cut accents (Plaid); acrylic paint; Lainie Day font (Internet download); Pea Cammi-pea font (Two Peas in a Bucket)

PowerAde 53
Cardstock; patterned paper (BasicGrey); chipboard letters (Li'l Davis); chipboard accents (Deluxe Designs, Making Memories); rub-on accent (Autumn Leaves); brads; solvent ink; pen; AL Worn Machine font (Internet download)

Before Forty 54
Cardstock; patterned paper (My Mind's Eye, Scenic Route); chipboard and plastic letters (Heidi Swapp); circle cutter; corner rounder; solvent ink; thread; Tasklist font (Internet download)

Vet 55
Cardstock; patterned paper (CherryArte); chipboard letters and shapes (Pressed Petals); brads; flowers (Prima); ribbon (Offray); word label (Paper Loft); dye ink; sandpaper; pen; Garamouche font (Internet download)

So I've Been Thinking 55
Patterned paper (American Crafts, BasicGrey, CherryArte); letter stamps (Making Memories); letter stickers (BasicGrey); acrylic paint; rickrack; solvent ink; staples; transparency

Five 57
Cardstock; chipboard letters and number, patterned paper (Scenic Route); brads (Queen & Co.); rub-on accents (7gypsies, Autumn Leaves); dye and solvent ink; pen; sandpaper; Essential font (Internet download)

Scooters 58
Cardstock; patterned paper (Adorn It, Crate Paper); chipboard letters (Pressed Petals); transparent letters (Heidi Swapp); chipboard shapes (Maya Road); acrylic paint; pen; Lucida Sans, Times New Roman fonts (Microsoft)

Crazy World 59
Cardstock; patterned paper (BasicGrey, Junkitz); mesh (Magic Mesh); chipboard letters (Li'l Davis); letter stickers (BasicGrey); acrylic paint; dimensional paint; corner rounder; dye ink; thread; Century Gothic font (Microsoft)

Growing Too Big 61
Cardstock; patterned paper (Cosmo Cricket, Fancy Pants); chipboard letters, letter stamps (Li'l Davis); chipboard stars (Heidi Swapp); ribbon (We R Memory Keepers); acrylic paint; pigment ink; corner rounder; thread; Maiandra GD (Internet download)

Thirty-Seven 62
Patterned paper (BasicGrey, CherryArte); chipboard letters (Everlasting Keepsakes); rub-on letters (American Crafts); buttons (unknown); ribbon (Heidi Grace); acrylic paint; dye ink; pen; Hot Chocolate font (Two Peas in a Bucket)

There's No Such Place As Far Away 63
Patterned paper (BasicGrey); chipboard shapes (Technique Tuesday); rub-on letters (Making Memories); buttons (ScrapArts); chalk ink; pen

Big Wide World 63
Patterned paper, chipboard accent (CherryArte); rub-on accents (CherryArte, Heidi Swapp); flowers (Prima); chalk ink; beads, sequins (unknown); canvas paper; pen; thread; Pegsanna font (Internet download)

Spring Blossoms 67
Cardstock; patterned paper (Autumn Leaves, BasicGrey, Three Bugs in a Rug); chipboard and rub-on letters (Scenic Route); chipboard accent (Delish Designs); buttons (Autumn Leaves); flowers (Li'l Davis, Prima); stamps (Autumn Leaves, Technique Tuesday); glitter glue; solvent ink; thread; pen; Tahoma font (Microsoft)

Good Times 68
Cardstock; patterned paper (Urban Lily); chipboard letters (Heidi Swapp); chipboard accents (BasicGrey); flowers, letter stickers (Doodlebug); rub-on accents (EK Success); brads (Bazzill); pen

Close Distance 69
Cardstock; patterned paper (ANW Crestwood, We R Memory Keepers); chipboard letters (Li'l Davis); rub-on letters (Making Memories); ribbon (May Arts); fabric tabs (Scrapworks); flowers (American Traditional, Queen & Co.); corner rounder; dye ink; Century Gothic font (Microsoft); LainieDaySH title font (Internet download)

Neighbour 69
Cardstock; chipboard letters (Heidi Swapp); rub-on accents (Autumn Leaves); corner rounder; pen; solvent ink; thread

Carbo Girl 71
Patterned paper (Three Bugs in a Rug); chipboard letters, rickrack (Li'l Davis); rub-on letters (Making Memories); brads (Queen & Co.); rhinestone circles (Heidi Swapp); solvent ink; Pea Amy font (Internet download)

Joker Genetics 72
Patterned paper (BasicGrey, Chatterbox, Fontwerks, Rusty Pickle); chipboard letters (Pressed Petals); transparent letters (Heidi Swapp); rub-on accents (K&Co., KI Memories); chipboard shapes (Bazzill); acrylic paint; flourish accent (Autumn Leaves); snaps (Chatterbox); MA Flirty font (Internet download)

Competitive 73
Cardstock; patterned paper (American Crafts, CherryArte); chipboard letters (BasicGrey); chipboard squares (unknown); pigment ink; pen

Always True Friends 75
Photos by: Lianne Gray, Pukekohe, New Zealand
Patterned paper (BasicGrey, Fancy Pants); embroidered fabric (Tarisota); chipboard letters (Heidi Swapp); corner rounder; decoupage medium; pen; sequins; solvent ink; Pea Johanna Script font (Internet download)

The Man Mind 76
Cardstock; patterned paper (Scenic Route); chipboard letters (Heidi Swapp); rub-on letters (American Crafts); buttons; solvent ink; thread; pen; My Own Topher font (Internet download)

Something I Can Always Count On 77
Cardstock; patterned paper (A2Z Essentials); chipboard letters (Heidi Swapp, Urban Lily); rub-on letters (Chatterbox, EK Success); chipboard accent (Fancy Pants); flower (Queen & Co.); brads (Bazzill); pen

Trash 2 Treasure 77
Cardstock; patterned paper (BasicGrey, My Mind's Eye); chipboard letters (Heidi Swapp, Scenic Route); chipboard accents (Collections Elements); buttons (SEI); colored pencils; pen; image editing software; Cheryl font (Internet download)

Supply List (continued)

10 Reasons 81
Cardstock; patterned paper (Crate Paper); letter and number stickers (Arctic Frog); number stamps (Autumn Leaves); brads (Queen & Co.); rub-on accents (Junkitz); pigment ink; AL Worn Machine font (Internet download)

Faithful Friend 82
Cardstock; patterned paper (BasicGrey, Scrapworks); letter stickers (American Crafts, Deluxe Designs); corner rounder; pen; solvent ink

Feijoa Tree 83
Cardstock; patterned paper (Crate Paper, Fancy Pants); chipboard letters (Li'l Davis, Scenic Route); letter stamps (PSX); rub-on accents (BasicGrey); corner rounder; pen; solvent ink; My Own Topher font (Internet download)

Wildlife 83
Cardstock; patterned paper (Crate Paper); letter stickers (Sonburn); date stickers (EK Success); tab (K&Co.); flowers (Prima); brads (Making Memories); thread; Century Gothic font (Microsoft); Lainie Day title font (Internet download)

Warriors 85
Cardstock; patterned paper (BasicGrey, CherryArte, Fancy Pants); chipboard letters (Pressed Petals); star brads (Queen & Co.); corner rounder; pen; solvent ink; thread; Tasklist font (Two Peas in a Bucket)

Trademe Addict 86
Cardstock; patterned paper (Scenic Route); transparent letters (Heidi Swapp); chipboard accents (Deluxe Designs); gesso; hole punch; notebook paper; solvent ink; pen

Pokemon 87
Cardstock; letter stickers (American Crafts); rub-on letters (Making Memories); buttons (unknown); acrylic paint; pen; Hot Chocolate font (Two Peas in a Bucket)

Blue Tab Explosion 87
Cardstock; patterned paper (BasicGrey, Scenic Route, We R Memory Keepers); chipboard letters (Heidi Swapp); chipboard accent (Deluxe Designs); rub-on accents and letters (American Crafts, Doodlebug); buttons (Autumn Leaves); pen; solvent ink; thread; Snowshoe font (Internet download)

Girlfriends 89
Cardstock; patterned paper (Scenic Route); chipboard accents (Deluxe Designs, Everlasting Keepsakes); rub-on letters (Dèjá Views); rub-on accents (Autumn Leaves); mask, ribbon (Heidi Swapp); rhinestone, trim (Making Memories); acrylic paint; pen; solvent ink; staples; Century Gothic font (Microsoft)

Best Friend 90
Chipboard letters, flowers, patterned paper (Chatterbox); corner rounder; pen

Scrap at Home Mum 91
Cardstock; patterned paper (BasicGrey, CherryArte); chipboard letters and accent (Scenic Route); rub-on letters (Creative Imaginations); beads (Queen & Co.); corner rounder; glass finish (Plaid); pen; solvent ink; Century Gothic font (Microsoft)

Easy 95
Chipboard, patterned paper (Scenic Route); letter stamps (Ma Vinci); rub-on letters (Making Memories); sandpaper; solvent ink; thread; Pea Lacy font (Kevin and Amanda)

Beautiful 96
Patterned paper (BasicGrey); chipboard letters (Li'l Davis); rub-on accents (7gypsies); brads (American Crafts); photo corners (Heidi Swapp); solvent ink; Red Dog font (Internet download)

Enjoy Her While She Is Young 97
Cardstock; patterned paper (Scenic Route); chipboard letters, flowers (Heidi Swapp); letter stamps (PSX); rub-on letters (Dee's Designs, Making Memories); rub-on accents, tags (BasicGrey); ribbon (American Crafts, Heidi Swapp, Making Memories); corner rounder; solvent ink; Pea AngeDawn font (Kevin and Amanda)

Can You See Me Now? 97
Cardstock; patterned paper (American Crafts); photo corners, transparent letters (Heidi Swapp); circle punch; pen; pigment ink; stamp (unknown)

To Be Free 99
Cardstock; patterned paper (Crate Paper); letter stickers (American Crafts, Imagination Project); chipboard accents (Everlasting Keepsakes); acrylic paint; solvent ink; Hot Chocolate font (Two Peas in a Bucket)

Courage 100
Photo by: Jennifer Creamer Berglund
Patterned paper (Creative Imaginations, Fancy Pants, Scenic Route); transparent letters (Heidi Swapp); chipboard accent (CherryArte); tags (Fancy Pants, Melissa Frances); ribbon (Fancy Pants); lace (unknown); thread; watermark ink; Rickety font (Two Peas in a Bucket)

Finding Me 101
Cardstock; buttons, patterned paper (SEI); chipboard letters (Pressed Petals); chipboard accents (Maya Road); acrylic paint; letter stickers (unknown); Americana BT brackets, Myriad Condensed Web journaling font (Internet downloads)

Caffeine O'clock 103
Photos by: Braden Howard, Pukekohe, New Zealand
Cardstock; chipboard letters, patterned paper (We R Memory Keepers); clock image (unknown); transparency; pen; AL Gettysburg, My Own Topher fonts (Internet download)

Set a Challenge 104
Photo by: Braden Howard, Pukekohe, New Zealand
Cardstock; patterned paper (BasicGrey, We R Memory Keepers); chipboard letters (Heidi Swapp); letter stickers (American Crafts); chipboard accents (Everlasting Keepsakes); stamps (Rhonna Designs); brads, flowers, photo turns (Queen & Co.); solvent ink; lace (unknown); Pea Lyndel font (Kevin and Amanda)

I Admit 105
Photo by: Paul Howard, Pukekohe, New Zealand
Patterned paper (BasicGrey); chipboard letters (Heidi Swapp); acrylic paint; solvent ink; thread; transparency; Tasklist font (Two Peas in a Bucket)

Obsessed 105
Photo by: Braden Howard, Pukekohe, New Zealand
Cardstock; patterned paper (Imagination Project); chipboard letters (Heidi Swapp); chipboard accent (Everlasting Keepsakes); beads, brads, flowers (Queen & Co.); vellum (Hot Off The Press); pen; thread

Thoughts from the Contributing Artists

Linda Albrecht *St. Peter, Minnesota*

The little things in life are what make up my favorite days. When I apply this concept to scrapbooking, the simple joys and words once spoken will be captured forever on my pages. From my own childhood, I remember things like the pancakes with chocolate chip smiles that my mom would make for special occasions. Those are really the extraordinary things of life that make us who we are—people growing, caring, and loving together as we look forward to making happy tomorrows with all of the little shared moments.

Jessie Baldwin *Las Vegas, Nevada*

When I go through my grandmother's albums, I don't look for perfect hair or beautiful clothes. I don't even look for perfect facial expressions. I look for the story. I look for the Flokati rug on the floor and the old car in the driveway. I look for the toys in the background and those crazy crocheted sweaters and potholders. I look for evidence of real life. I want to know and remember the everyday things that my family experienced. What was on the dinner table? What images defined that era? What caused someone to bring out a camera at that moment? Those are the things that I investigate. Because of this, I want to be sure my own albums tell that story as well.

Marieke Broekman *Wellington, New Zealand*

Contributing to **That's Life** has had a dramatic impact on how and what I scrapbook. I want to record the everyday, the ordinary and extraordinary things that shape our days and lives. It has caused me to look at these moments as something worth remembering. I still scrapbook the tribute pages, the events and celebrations, but I now keep a little notebook to jot down ideas when they strike me as we go about our daily routine. If I don't document the little details, they'll soon be forgotten.

Kelly Goree *Shelbyville, Kentucky*

I've often told my mom that I can remember very early childhood events, even down to vivid descriptions of what I was wearing and where we were. But she always contradicts me and tells me that it's the photographs I've seen of those events that have given me these "memories," and perhaps she's right. It's those photos of the daily snippets of life that make them memorable even years later. I want my scrapbook pages to do the same thing for my children that those photos did for me. I want the photos and layouts to bring their story to life, not just for them but for their children after them.

Loretta Grayson *Emu Vale, Queensland, Australia*

When I was child, now and then my parents would set up the slide projector and we would have a Slide Night. It was a great time to revisit the places we had been, listen to favorite family stories and have a giggle at the old-fashioned things in some of the photos. Our scrapbooks are like those old Slide Nights. We look through them to relive the small things that make our family special. The photos help us remember the unique story our family has attached to that memory. My next project will be to create a layout for each family member, documenting those infamous moments that are brought up regularly and laughed about at family get-togethers. They may be small stories to the outside world, but to us they are the stuff of legends.

Caro Huot *Laval, Quebec, Canada*

I've always enjoyed capturing life's everyday moments. But this project really made me think outside the box, to document not only the moments, but also my feelings about those moments. I scrapbook little things that I want my kids to remember, as silly or trivial as the subject may seem at the moment. How I wish my mother had done something similar for me. Since my parents died when I was a teen, I am left with many questions. I wish I remembered more moments from my childhood, that I knew how my parents felt about life. Were they as close to their sisters as I am to mine? What did they think we would grow up to become? Did they have dreams they pushed aside to become parents? By scrapbooking the everyday moments and thoughts, you are leaving a legacy that is worth more than you can imagine.

Adrienne Looman *San Diego, California*

When scrapbooking, I used to always concentrate on the "big picture"— big events in life, big changes, etc. Now I realize, after doing these layouts, that there's just as much meaning and enjoyment in the little things. Now I'm going to scrapbook more things about work in the military, so I can remember what was discussed and how I felt. I also plan to scrapbook some of the flowers that I've photographed in San Diego. I want my layouts to reflect both the big and little things in life.

Amelia McIvor *Melbourne, Victoria, Australia*

One of the joys of scrapbooking is taking a tiny part of the day, a memory or a quirk, and recording it for future reference. When we scrap about these details, we create a way for others to see who we really are, a legacy for our family and future generations. I love to show these everyday pages to my parents and grandparents, and listen to stories about their day-to-day life when they were my age. Hopefully this tradition will continue with my children. I now realize that scrapping my daily life is just as important as scrapping the big events. From now on I plan to take more inspiration from the everyday.

Lisa VanderVeen *Mendham, New Jersey*

It's easy to remember the big things—getting married, graduating from college and law school, the birth of our child. Those events are indelibly burned into our brains. But the little things are so easily forgotten, yet crucial for telling our complete story. I wish I had a scrapbook of my childhood that answered questions such as, "What meals did my mom make on a regular basis? What was my morning routine before school?" It's the tiny moments that make up our days and years. Working on this book reminded me to capture the little things that I want to remember in years to come.

Courtney Walsh *Winnebago, Illinois*

I think these everyday moments are the stuff of life. I hope these moments are what I will really remember—the overflowing toilet and the tormented bugs—the little things that make my days funny and memorable. I love to scrapbook big events too, but it seems I'm always finding the moments in the middle of the chaos. That's what I hold onto. Because life is really made up of moments, right? And I want to remember them all!

Evana Willis *Mapua, Nelson Bays, New Zealand*

It is the things we overlook and do daily that make up our everyday life. The layouts that I created for **That's Life** were not a challenge for me. As a family, we do random things every day that are not sweet or perfect. Our life is not all pigtails and polka dots. This project was unconventional and thought provoking. I'm sure the topic for my next layout is lurking just around the corner. Now I will truly look at things with less expectations and more realism. After all, "that's life."

Source Guide

The following companies manufacture products featured in this book. Please check your local retailers to find these materials, or go to a company's Web site for the latest product. In addition, we have made every attempt to properly credit the items mentioned in this book. We apologize to any company that we have listed incorrectly, and would appreciate hearing from you.

7 Gypsies
(877) 749-7797
www.sevengypsies.com

A2Z Essentials
(419) 663-2869
www.geta2z.com

Adorn It / Carolee's Creations
(435) 563-1100
www.adornit.com

American Crafts
(801) 226-0747
www.americancrafts.com

American Traditional Designs
(800) 448-6656
www.americantraditional.com

ANW Crestwood
(973) 406-5000
www.anwcrestwood.com

Arctic Frog
(479) 636-3764
www.arcticfrog.com

Autumn Leaves
(800) 588-6707
www.autumnleaves.com

BasicGrey
(801) 544-1116
www.basicgrey.com

Bazzill Basics Paper
(480) 558-8557
www.bazzillbasics.com

Berwick Offray, LLC
(800) 344-5533
www.offray.com

Chatterbox, Inc.
(888) 416-6260
www.chatterboxinc.com

Cherry Arte
(212) 465-3495
www.cherryarte.com

Collections Elements
www.bumblebeecrafts.com.au

Cosmo Cricket
(800) 852-8810
www.cosmocricket.com

Crafter's Workshop, The
(877) 272-3837
www.thecraftersworkshop.com

Crate Paper
(702) 966-0409
www.cratepaper.com

Creative Imaginations
(800) 942-6487
www.cigift.com

Daisy D's Paper Company
(888) 601-8955
www.daisydspaper.com

Dee's Designs
http://vij10.tripod.com/deesdesigns

Dèjá Views
(800) 243-8419
www.dejaviews.com

Delish Designs
(360) 897-1254
www.delishdesigns.com

Deluxe Designs
(480) 497-9005
www.deluxecuts.com

Doodlebug Design Inc.
(877) 800-9190
www.doodlebug.ws

EK Success, Ltd.
(800) 524-1349
www.eksuccess.com

Everlasting Keepsakes by faith
(816) 896-7037
www.everlastinkeepsakes.com

Fancy Pants Designs, LLC
(801) 779-3212
www.fancypantsdesigns.com

FiberMark
(802) 257-0365
www.fibermark.com

Fiber Scraps
(215) 230-4905
www.fiberscraps.com

Fontwerks
(604) 942-3105
www.fontwerks.com

Greener Pastures
www.greenerpastures.co.nz

Heidi Grace Designs, Inc.
(866) 348-5661
www.heidigrace.com

Heidi Swapp/Advantus Corporation
(904) 482-0092
www.heidiswapp.com

Hot Off The Press, Inc.
(800) 227-9595
www.b2b.hotp.com

Imagination Project, Inc.
(888) 477-6532
www.imaginationproject.com

Junkitz
(732) 792-1108
www.junkitz.com

K&Company
(888) 244-2083
www.kandcompany.com

Kevin and Amanda
www.geocities.com/fontsforpeas

KI Memories
(972) 243-5595
www.kimemories.com

Lazar Studiowerx, Inc.
(866) 478-9379
www.lazarstudiowerx.com

Li'l Davis Designs
(480) 223-0080
www.lildavisdesigns.com

Little Black Dress Designs
(360) 897-8844
www.littleblackdressdesigns.com

Ma Vinci's Reliquary
www.reliquary.cyberstamps.com

Magic Mesh
(651) 345-6374
www.magicmesh.com

Making Memories
(801) 294-0430
www.makingmemories.com

May Arts
(800) 442-3950
www.mayarts.com

Maya Road, LLC
(214) 488-3279
www.mayaroad.com

me & my BiG ideas
(949) 583-2065
www.meandmybigideas.com

Melissa Frances/Heart & Home, Inc.
(888) 616-6166
www.melissafrances.com

Microsoft Corporation
www.microsoft.com

My Mind's Eye, Inc.
(866) 989-0320
www.mymindseye.com

Office Max
www.officemax.com

Offray- see Berwick Offray, LLC

Paper Loft, The
(801) 254-1961
www.paperloft.com

Plaid Enterprises, Inc.
(800) 842-4197
www.plaidonline.com

Pressed Petals
(800) 748-4656
www.pressedpetals.com

Prima Marketing, Inc.
(909) 627-5532
www.primamarketinginc.com

PSX Design
www.sierra-enterprises.com/psxmain

Queen & Co.
(858) 613-7858
www.queenandcompany.com

Rhonna Designs
www.rhonnadesigns.com

Rusty Pickle
(801) 746-1045
www.rustypickle.com

Scenic Route Paper Co.
(801) 225-5754
www.scenicroutepaper.com

ScrapArts
(503) 631-4893
www.scraparts.com

Scrapworks, LLC / As You Wish Products, LLC
(801) 363-1010
www.scrapworks.com

SEI, Inc.
(800) 333-3279
www.shopsei.com

Sonburn, Inc.
(800) 436-4919
www.sonburn.com

Strano Designs
(508) 454-4615
www.stranodesigns.com

Tarisota Collections
www.tarisota.com.au

Technique Tuesday, LLC
(503) 644-4073
www.techniquetuesday.com

Three Bugs in a Rug, LLC
(801) 804-6657
www.threebugsinarug.com

Two Peas in a Bucket
(888) 896-7327
www.twopeasinabucket.com

Urban Lily
www.urbanlily.com

We R Memory Keepers, Inc.
(801) 539-5000
www.weronthenet.com

Index

Check out these other scrapbooking titles from Memory Makers Books!

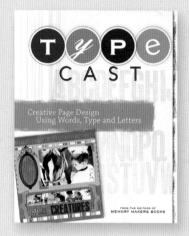

Type Cast

Combining simple techniques with inspiring artwork, Type Cast will teach you how to get the most out of your tools, supplies and even your own handwriting to create fabulous pages that fully integrate text into successful designs.

ISBN-13: 978-1-59963-003-8
ISBN-10: 1-59963-003-6
Paperback
128 pages
Z0695

Focal Point

Add that extra punch of visual creativity through the use of hands-on altering techniques! From creative ways to crop to photo transfer ideas to using images printed on unique surfaces, this book offers the latest trends for showing off your treasured photos.

ISBN-13: 978-1-892127-96-9
ISBN-10: 1-892127-96-2
Paperback
128 pages
Z0530

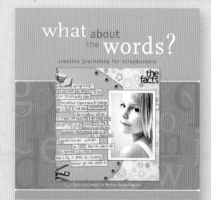

What About the Words?

Over 30 unique journaling formats and page after page of great layouts will inspire scrapbookers to record their own memories and experiences in the most engaging and expressive ways possible.

ISBN-13: 978-1-892127-77-8
ISBN-10: 1-892127-77-6
Paperback
128 pages
Z0017

These books and other fine Memory Makers titles are available at your local scrapbook or craft store, bookstore or from online suppliers, including **www.memorymakersmagazine.com**.